California Journal

"Edgar Morin has written an engaging journal about his trip from Paris to California in the tumultuous years of 1969 and 1970. Along the way this Frenchman learns about American youth who were generating their own counter-culture, reading their own free press, participating in their own unscripted revolution. A middle-aged philosopher, Morin worked at the Salk Institute in La Jolla, California, and comments on everything from race relations to physico-chemical-biological systemology to Billy Graham. His journey takes him to a Los Angeles Park-In, where he is mystified by a young girl's smile, to communes outside of San Francisco, where he considers the emerging cultural revolution, and into the homes and thoughts of Jonas Salk and Herbert Marcuse. Along the way Morin contemplates the evolving scene of the late 1960s, from adolescence to love to utopia. And in months, America had changed him: 'Since I've been here,' he wrote, 'I've been intellectually high.' He also discovered personal freedom: 'At the age of forty-eight, I'm learning how to live!' Come along, enjoy this trip; it's not to be missed."

TERRY H. ANDERSON, author of
The Movement and the Sixties,
and *The Sixties*

"Scanning America like a modern de Tocqueville, Morin's personal meditations on the tumultuous sixties are filled with acute insights."

PHILIP SLATER, author of
The Pursuit of Loneliness
and *A Dream Deferred*

California Journal

EDGAR MORIN

Translated by
Deborah Cowell

sussex
ACADEMIC
PRESS

Brighton • Portland

2 4 6 8 10 9 7 5 3

First published in 2008 by
SUSSEX ACADEMIC PRESS
PO Box 139
Eastbourne BN24 9BP

and in the United States of America by
SUSSEX ACADEMIC PRESS
920 NE 58th Ave Suite 300
Portland, Oregon 97213-3786

British Library Cataloguing in Publication Data
A CIP catalogue record for this book is available from the British Library.

Library of Congress Cataloging-in-Publication Data
Morin, Edgar.
[Journal de Californie. English]
California journal / Edgar Morin ; translated by Deborah Cowell.
p. cm.
Includes bibliographical references.
"First published in French by Editions du Seuil in 1970."
ISBN 978-1-84519-275-4 (pb : alk. paper)
1. California—Description and travel. 2. Morin, Edgar—Travel—California. 3. California--Social life and customs—20th century. 4. Popular culture—California—History—20th century. 5. Social change—California—History—20th century. 6. California—Social conditions—20th century. 7. California—Intellectual life—20th century.
I. Title.
F866.2.M6513 2008
917.9404′53—dc22

2007047676

Mixed Sources
Product group from well-managed forests and other controlled sources
www.fsc.org Cert no. SGS-COC-2482
© 1996 Forest Stewardship Council
FSC

Typeset and designed by SAP, Brighton & Eastbourne.
Printed by TJ International, Padstow, Cornwall.
This book is printed on acid-free paper.

Contents

Contents

Contents

Contents

Foreword by Alfonso Montuori

THE SIXTIES

A decade that was undoubtedly of remarkable cultural and political significance for the 20th century. Perhaps no decade elicits such polarized responses. As the sociologist Philip Slater points out, on the Left it can often be idealized, a golden age from the perspective of the 21st century's gloomy economic and political first decade. An age of creativity, love, music, revolution, freedom.

In the US, the Right has steadfastly refused to see any redeeming value in the Sixties. It represents the beginning of the end, an era that marked the great decay of western civilization, leading to Nihilism, Post-modernism, Anti-Americanism, flag-burning, drug use, and the collapse of the family, among other things. In the media, more often than not the Sixtiesy are portrayed, like most everything else, sensationally, with a hint of sarcasm and a lot of focus on – of course – drugs and sex.

A decade that arouses such polarizing views must surely deserve to be revisited, studied, understood better. It was an enormously complex era, a truly transitional one, and its interpretation and the lessons we can learn from it are significant in terms of the way we think of our future. Perhaps this is why the reflections of a thinker associated with complexity, with an unwillingness to polarize and in the process paint over-simplified, mutilating black-and-white interpretations interpretations, is particularly significant at this point.

In 1969, Edgar Morin, a 48 year-old French sociologist with a number of significant publications behind him on subjects ranging from Death to Cinema (Morin, 2005a, 2005b) to the sociology of Modernization (Morin, 1970), and whose "sociology of the present" foreshadowed today's blossoming interest in Action Research (Morin, 1971), flew to San Diego to spend a year at the Salk Center. It proved to be a turning point for many different reasons.

In California Morin was exposed to systems theory, cybernetics, and information theory that were to deeply influence his future work and culminate in his magnum opus *Method*. The main thrust of these two volumes was to develop a form of thinking and inquiry that can account for complexity, ambiguity, and uncertainty, something traditional scientific thinking, with its focus on laws, objectivity, and "clear and distinct ideas," was unable to do (Morin, 1981, 1985, 1986, 2008). Already in *L'Homme et la Mort* (Humanity and Death) Morin had taken a multidisciplinary approach, seeking to gain a fuller understanding of the subject than any one single discipline could provide. Perhaps the single most important impetus behind the so-called "transversal" sciences of systems theory and cybernetics had been to provide a language with which to study dynamic wholes across disciplines. Steeped in Marx and Hegel, with their focus on wholes and on dialectics, Morin found in the systems/cybernetic perspective a strong resonance, a way of thinking that was free of the ideological, political baggage that he had so famously rejected in the early Fifties.

For Morin, the experience of the Sixties in California connected a number of key points that were, and continue to be, central to his work. They include the unexpected, the role of uncertainty in life and in world events. Paris '68 was unexpected, as was more generally the outpouring of the Sixties revolution. It had not been predicted; it was a singular *event* – and such singular events were not accounted for in the sociology of the times, which stressed statistically measurable lawlike regularities. Morin the sociologist was very critical of a sociology that focused only on regularities, not on singular events and crises. For Morin those were precisely the opportunities to gain a deeper understanding of any social system.

Max Weber's term *Statu Nascenti*, or nascent state, refers to those moments when a social movement has just come together, filled with excitement and possibility. The Italian sociologist Francesco Alberoni has applied this term both to incipient social movements and to falling in love – those times when we are living in a world rich with possibilities, with potential, with, again, the unexpected (Alberoni, 1989, 2004). Reading Morin's experience in California we see that this experience of the nascent state is very dear to him, that it carries both an emotional charge as he witnesses the potential both in the Sixties' political, social, and cultural revolution, and in the interactions he has with individuals, particularly women. We see, in fact, a nascent state both socially and personally.

This brings us to yet another key aspect of Morin's work – the inextricable presence of the observer in the observation. Morin is not some distant, aloof observer with a pipe and a notepad, a social scientist studying a foreign culture. On the contrary – the *California Journal* begins with Morin's immensely frustrating experience at the airport on the way to the US, an experience that travelers today can relate to with little difficulty. In an almost Fellini-esque account of his fantasies of vengeance towards the airline, Morin is clearly setting the tone. He is not a detached scientist here. He is a human being who is in the world, drawn into its petty irritations and not ashamed to express his delight or disgust with human interactions.

The popular accounts of European intellectuals in the US, from Eco to Baudrillard to Levy, all have a sense of detachment and irony which sometimes borders on the smug. Morin is all there, and if anything he presents himself in ways that are remarkably vulnerable. His occasional outbursts of joy and his admission that in the exuberance and vitality of '69, at 48 years old he has finally learned to live, may strike some as about as far removed from the detachment of a social scientist or from postmodern irony as one could get. His irritations, confusion, anger, the way he writes about the US to a friend and then on reflection finds himself repeating all the European clichés about the US, and the way he is often captivated by the charm of a beautiful woman, are all accounted for in this decidedly non-academic narrative.

But at the same time that Morin is telling us about being distracted by a beautiful woman's face, we also find in this volume an enormous series of insights into his experience and his analysis of the US during this complex time. And the two may well be related. Morin does not compartmentalize the academic and the personal: he is *both* a scholar and a human being, and the two inform each other. Morin reminds us that the scientific academic expert is also a human being, a father, or a sister, somebody who does the shopping, raises children and is somebody's son/daughter/neighbor/friend. Does the academic role and experience inform the person's life in any way? For Morin, the separation is unacceptable. The "objective" scientist becomes a very "subjective" mother, father, daughter, son, grocery shopper, neighbor, etc.

The Morin of this *Journal* is the Morin who argues insistently that the sociologist must be incorporated in sociology, the observer in the observation. Morin is a participant in this exploration of California. He is not detached, objective, removed, whether through "scientific objectivity" or "detached irony." He's living the experience, with all its joys and all its suffering.

REFLECTIONS FROM THE 21ST CENTURY

This book is being published in 2008, the 40th anniversary of Paris '68. Morin chronicled the events of '68 in his articles in *Le Monde*, sympathetic to the unexpected outburst of change, the tearing down of old structures, the outburst of hope and optimism, and the critique of stultifying systems (Morin, Lefort, & Castoriadis, 1968). For Morin, a crisis also allows insight into the deep structures of a system as its underlying structures and assumptions are brought to the fore (Morin, 1993). The events of '68 therefore provided a unique opportunity to study an event, something that traditional sociology with its quantophrenic tendencies could not account for: an unexpected, dramatic, *singular* moment that was the result of unpredictable forces.

Morin sees great potential for hope in the unexpected. He recognizes the role of the unexpected, the ambiguous, the uncertain to a greater extent than just about any major thinker today. And the unexpected, while it is staring us in the face, is still largely left out of public discourse which tends to see the future as linear and thinks of the unexpected mostly in terms of natural catastrophes. At the same time, he does not see it as a weakness, as the result of social science's inability to predict, as a deplorable but inevitable lack of order. Like a jazz musician, Morin sees the unexpected, the *improvisus*, as an opportunity for creativity and improvisation, for living life in the moment with the material and the experience we are confronted with.

In 1983 I began my graduate studies in International Relations. If at that time I had told my instructors that in less than ten years there would be no Soviet Union, that within 25 years China and India would be major international economic forces and the Euro – born of those boring Eurocrats that at the time were so roundly dismissed as symbols of decaying and increasingly marginal old Europe – would make it very expensive for Americans to travel in Europe, I would have been laughed out of the school. The expectation was that US–Soviet nuclear gun-pointing would either outlive us all, or kill us all.

How to account for this change – and its rapidity? How can we even begin to think about a world that undergoes such dramatic and unexpected changes? This is a key issue: the way we have been taught to think is itself problematic. It doesn't allow us to make sense of unexpected, complex phenomena. And what does that really mean?

We have seen the argument that the Sixties are deeply polarizing – despised by many on the Right, idealized by many on the Left. What is lost in this polarization is the complexity of the events themselves. It's "you're either for the Sixties or against them" binary oppositions that we find in the "you're either for us or against us" statements that likewise preclude any serious, thoughtful assessment of a situation and reduce it to black and white. Morin has always rejected facile polarization. When it was popular among intellectuals to portray popular culture as the opium of the masses, Morin's studies of popular culture showed them in all their complexity, and recognized that they did in fact have something to offer – that in fact they played a central role in the social imaginary (Morin, 2005b; Mortimer, 2001). Morin was viciously attacked by Pierre Bourdieu, for whom popular culture was, predictably, "an instrument of alienation at the service of capitalism to divert the proletariat from its revolutionary mission" (Mortimer, 2001, p. 78). Morin has always avoided such ideological stands, and in hindsight Morin's work stands the test of time and Bourdieu's parroting of the party line clearly does not.

At the time, Morin had to deal with the insults that came with not being perceived as "taking a stand," when in fact he was pointing out the pitfalls of such black and white thinking, and the way it would, inevitably, lead to an impoverished and unwise course of action that above all did not allow for dissent and differences of opinion. In that sense, Morin has always been very anti-authoritarian. But his complex perspective illuminates how anti-authoritarianism itself can become a rigid doctrine and an authoritarian belief system.

Already in this *Journal* we find Morin reflecting on the bankruptcy of Left and Right, and the forces that may lead to the need for a radically different discourse and configuration of political perspectives. The volume is filled with such insights and opportunities for reflection. The fact that they are based on experiences and movements emerging forty years ago is particularly poignant. *California Journal*'s re-issue on the anniversary of Paris '68, and almost 40 years after Morin's visit to California, is very timely. It contains reflections, premonitions, and a way of thinking that cast considerable light on California and the US today, and offer us a different and generative way of thinking about the challenges that lie ahead.

ALFONSO MONTUORI
California Institute of Integral Studies
San Francisco
April 2008

References

Alberoni, F. (1989). *Genesi. Come si creano i miti, i valori, le istituzioni della civiltà occidentale. [Genesis. How the myths, values, and institutions of western soceity were created.]*. Milano: Garzanti.

—— (2004). *Il mistero dell'innamoramento. [The mystery of falling in love.]*. Milano: Rizzoli.

Morin, E. (1970). *The red and the white. Report from a French village*. New York: Pantheon Books.

—— (1971). *Rumor in Orleans*. New York: Blond.

—— (1981). *La méthode. 1. La nature de la nature [Method. volume 1. The nature of nature]*. Paris: Seuil.

—— (1985). *La Méthode, tome 2. La vie de la vie [Method, volume 2. The life of life]*. Paris: Seuil.

—— (1986). *La conoscenza della conoscenza. [Method, vol. 3. Knowledge of knowledge.]*. Milano: Feltrinelli.

—— (1993). For a crisiology. *Industrial & Environmental Crisis Quarterly*, 7, 5–22.

—— (2005a). *The stars*. Minneapolis: University of Minnesota Press.

—— (2005b). *The cinema, or the imaginary man.* Minneapolis: University of Minnesota Press.

—— (2008). *On Complexity.* Cresskill, NJ: Hampton Press.

——, Lefort, C., & Castoriadis, C. (1968). *Mai 1968 : la brèche : premières réflexions sur les événements [May 1968: The breach: First reflections on the events].* Paris: Fayard.

Mortimer, L. (2001). We are the dance: Cinema, death, and the imaginary in the thought of Edgar Morin. *Thesis Eleven,* 64 (77), 77–95.

For
John Hunt
Jacques Monod
Jonas Salk

Reintroduction
Fourteen Years Later

My *California Journal* is, of course, a journal about California, but it is also the journal of what happened to me in California, and what I think I learned or came to understand in California.

The journal is like a suspension containing micro-commentaries, sociology flashes, and meditations on things I saw, experienced, or read. On rereading it today, I recognize seeds of articles and books I was to write in the seventies, and it strikes me that I have yet to bring all the latent seeds from that period to fruition. When I handed over the book to my French publisher (Seuil) in June 1970, I decided to add a postscript to what I had written, describing the happiness which, thanks to an extraordinary combination of circumstances, was granted me that year in February.

All this may sound cobbled together and incongruous, but I think its unity lies in the vortex that sweeps up each element of this journal and makes communicate, or activates, three axes of reference. At one axis, there is California, and more broadly the United States, at that crucial moment in its history; at the second, my own life, in its most personal dimension, at a crucial point in my own history; the third is defined by the fundamental problems concerning Man, life and society which had never ceased to haunt me, and now began to demand even more of my attention, never to relinquish their hold on me. And so being catapulted into that "entranced" California gave a new tenor to my life, while my presence in the cloister-cum-observatory of the Salk Institute encouraged me to return to my research and to my quest. I had never felt so receptive to my environment: not only the sea, sky, birds, nature and cities of that fabulous land, but also the countless extraordinary and intensely moving manifestations of a "cultural revolution" in the Far West; I even enjoyed TV series and programs like *Star Trek* or the *Dean Martin Show*. I was both studying and living ardently, swept along in the vortex which took me from the life sciences to my own life, and from my life to Californian life, and it is that vortex which constitutes this journal.

The California of that time is not the same California to which I returned in 1981, and I am no longer the same man who spent a season in Arcadia . . .

What fascinated me at the time was not only that California was America's "brain," which it still is, in a different sense. It was the fact that, in California, America was giving birth to another America, perhaps even an anti-America (an anti-America which, as became clear from closer examination, sprang from the same deep mythological sources that first created the United States).

I arrived late in the day, in time to see the last, brightest flames, but also the first fading of the spectacular conflagration that had begun between 1963 and 1965 in Berkeley. I am someone who is always profoundly moved by nascent states and infant revolutions, when the ossified, rigid, oppressive and oppressing structures of conventional life break down. I am one of those who are always moved by the boundless hopes of the first crusades. I was enthralled, in the strong sense of the word, by the powerful undercurrent that swept along not only an entire generation of young people, but people of all ages, and carried them towards more fraternity, love, freedom and self-fulfillment . . . Rereading the notes for this journal, I see how far my enthusiasm lacked illusion, how emptiness loomed in the background to my enchantment; how uncertainty, tragedy and despair enveloped the kernel of happiness which I experienced and which I shared with those around me. Max Gallo's article on my book puts it very well: "the tragic nature of history is at the center of this happy book." Thus, I maintain that what is for me "the source of the true future revolution" is "still so rudimentary, so ill-equipped, without the apparatus that would allow them to tell the difference between true and false gospels." And: "This is just the first stage, which can only result in failure, and there will be more and more failures." And: "Between them, drug addiction and Marxism-Leninism (the other drug) are destroying the great crusade of love." And: "Perhaps all of this will come to nothing: the global crisis, and particularly that of the United States, makes regressive forms of evolution almost inevitable, and all these seeds will be mercilessly trampled before they can pass on the life within them." And: "It's all happening as if the end of the world had already come, as if they were rebuilding a Crusoe-esque civilization out of the debris from the shipwreck." And: "That's why they are so sad. They know that they are being murdered." My enthusiasm was all the more intense because I knew how very ephemeral, fragile, but unique, this moment of life was to be. As I experienced this "ecstasy of history" I was fully aware that that was what it was. Against a background of immediate despair, I projected my hope into the future: "However short a time it lasts, it has been lived through, it has existed; just as the first heart transplants, in the short time they survive before being rejected, show that it is possible to live *with a different heart.*"

Twelve years later, everything seems to have returned to normal. Of course, a few communes have survived, a few institutions remain. But the shock wave has died away. And yet a long wave has swept through every section of American society, reaching much further than in post-'68 France. The former proponents of the counter-culture, of the student revolt, and of the communes have been reintegrated into the worlds of research, universities, business, or careers; sometimes their ideas have veered towards Paleo-Hinduism or neo-liberalism. But they have taken with them into the diaspora some of the viruses from those fervent years. The generations under 40 are no longer quite like their predecessors. Their difference lies in that *je-ne-sais-quoi* which, as Jankelevitch says, is precisely what makes all the difference. American culture has "re-assimilated" the seemingly innocuous seeds of the counter-culture, but are these seeds really spent? In one sense, nothing has changed, and in another, everything has changed. It is in our relationships with ourselves, and with others, that each of us has changed a little, just as it is in its relationship with itself that the United States has changed a little . . . Is there still an opening, a breach, beneath what looks like a smoothly restored surface? Has the economic crisis suffocated the cultural crisis, or is the latter merely sleeping? I don't know, we shall see. In the meantime, the Californian brain is occupied with other things . . .

The return to Paris was hard. What had first moved me, then seemed natural, in California, was that aspiration, not only among young people, but, I repeat, among people of all ages – of my own age – to bring their ideas more closely in tune with their lives, and their lives with their ideas. I felt more strongly than ever how much life was despised by intellectuals back in France. The idea of life, here, was reactionary, and dangerous; vitalism was Nietzschean, fascistic; biology had to be kept separate from the human sciences, culture could only be conceived of in opposition to nature. And for our great theorists, abstract ideas still took priority over living reality. Among our intelligentsia, the disjunction between life and ideas was clearly the norm. Ideas were socialist, revolutionary, proletarian. Life was *petit bourgeois*, it was for civil servants; it was trivial, ritualistic, egotistical. I wrote in this journal that "at the age of forty-eight, I am learning how to live," which some found moving, but others found laughable. The latter kind of people do not question their lives, they have nothing to learn from life. They conceal their being within their doctrine. Their "I" is majestic, not confessional or humble. They hide their ambitions, their desires, their weaknesses, their delirium.

Still, my book was received with much less sarcasm than it might have been. The reason is that it was published two years after '68, at a time of anxiety, uncertainty, and questioning. Only the hyper-fanatics accused me of betraying the proletariat and the third world. Only the insanely abstract who would never have married a Black woman reproached me for ignoring the Blacks.

For my part, twelve years on, I realize that my time in California has been banished forever into the past, I see the happiness I never found again, but which has left its traces in me; I see myself on the one hand so different after all the sorrows and the joys that came later, after separations, and drifting, and yet still the same, still swept along by my ardor to learn, and investing my whole life in the enterprise which was gestating then in my unconscious: the drive to identify and attempt to rethink this search for a "method," which can and must now develop its kernel, if I succeed in finishing the *Connaissance de la connaisance.*[1]

E.M., April '83

The Beginning
September 1966

Crowds at Orly. With the deluge of holiday arrivals and departures, the beautiful, smooth-running airport, where once all was order, calm and beauty, has suddenly been reduced to a congested, panic-ridden, antiquated station. There are interminable queues in front of every check-in counter. Campers on charter holidays rub shoulders in the crowd with international celebrities and jet-setters. The row is deafening. People are blocking each other's way. A steward, noticing Johanne, directs us to a vacant first-class counter, where we pick up our coach class boarding passes. It's all too easy.

In the customs hall, we make a beeline for the tax-free shops, as if the secret reason for taking intercontinental flights was to buy cartons of cigarettes and alcohol at discount prices. We get six bottles, stopping there only because we can't carry any more. We're already weighed down like pack mules, with purses and backpacks, a briefcase and a typewriter, kept as hand luggage so the excess weight won't be counted against us. Johanne stops at the perfume shop to buy Cardin's *Singulier*. When, after the second call, we race up to the departure gate, and are surprised to see that the hall is empty. The flight attendants have already boarded the passengers, and they're all installed inside the Boeing which is standing right in front of us. And then one of the flight attendants announces:

"There's no more room."

Bewilderment, perspiration, collapse. *What*? The flight attendant, in the weary, irritated tone she reserves for those within range, that is, the victims (an old American-Marseillais couple, and Johanne and I), explains that there has been a mistake, and she is no more responsible for it than we are. I learn a new word, which seems to explain the whole thing in her eyes, and is supposed to calm us, but which in fact leaves us floundering in horror: "over-booking." It seems that the airplane has been "overbooked," which means that more tickets had been reserved than there were seats available. Is this a joke, or a computer's nervous breakdown? I'd rather believe that some mistake has been made at check-in, and I ask the flight attendant to find out. She answers, as if talking to a spoiled child, that it's quite impossible. The plane is due to leave in ten minutes. Precisely! The very thing that makes the least little action on her part pointless in her eyes makes it a matter of urgency in mine. I tell her that my luggage is on the plane, that I have a connecting flight in Los Angeles for San Diego, that people are expecting me there, that I *have* to be at my meeting. The two flight attendants put on distant expressions. I demand to see someone in charge. One of the flight attendants emerges from behind her little counter and says: "Follow me."

It's a trap. Instead of leading us to some manager or other, she takes us to the connections counter, and leaves us there. And here, flocked together, are all the people who have missed their connections, those who found the plane was full even though they'd reserved from Quito or New York, and Scandinavians or Asians who don't understand a word of French and as a result have no idea what's going on. A fat Germanic blonde erupts in terrifying screams. A Belgian-Latin American rolls his eyes heavenward, and chants, in four languages, articulating every syllable: "I have been waiting four hours at this counter."

We finally explain our case to a flight attendant who takes notes, but as it is three o'clock, and she's at the end of her shift, she goes looking for another flight attendant, who is supposed to draw up a new itinerary for us. Since everything seems to be booked up, instead of using her initiative and seeking out another combination on the same day with a rival Scandinavian airline, the flight attendant gives me a schedule for the following day, adding on another twelve hours, which brings it up to a total of twenty-four, changing planes in London, Chicago, and of course Los Angeles. The wait for the tickets nearly finishes me off. I'm still asking to see someone in charge, and finally they bring me a little steward who expresses vague regret and suggests I write to Air France. In the meantime, the injury I've suffered has grown considerably. At the outset, all I'd done was missed my connection, and let down the people who were supposed to be meeting me at the airport in San Diego. Then I announce that I am missing a very important scientific meeting. Then it becomes an international conference of such importance that the fate of the world practically seems to depend on it, and I only just manage to stop myself from making what's happening to me into a catastrophe of global proportions.

Only after an hour and a half of waiting, that is, too late, do productive ideas occur to me: first of all, I call J., who is somebody in Air France. He's away, but his secretary informs a boss at Orly who will come and find me. He comes, but too late, when they have already given me our new tickets. Another idea occurs to me, in retrospect: I should have insisted on speaking to the pilot of the plane. I imagine climbing up the stairway, addressing myself to the pilot, whose calm, manly face is like a cross between Mermoz and Saint-Exupéry, and who listens to me attentively; when I have finished my explanation, he simply says: "Climb aboard." I beckon to Johanne. We get on. The plane leaves. Saved! No, lost! We're still standing at the counter and the plane has irrevocably flown off without us.

All day long, I mull over my frustration at this missed plane, which had been right there, within reach, ready to welcome me aboard. Several times this image passes before my eyes, and, as if in a nightmare, I am immobilized, paralyzed, I can't manage to get on this plane, *my* plane. At the same time, I feel profound dissatisfaction, very cross with myself: I was taken by surprise, stunned; it took me two hours to realize, too late, what I should have done: speak to the pilot.

At the same time, too, a feeling of impotent rage is fermenting inside me, trying to focus on a guilty party, and to exact ferocious revenge. The guilty parties are the two flight attendants, who are looking uglier and more hypocritical by the minute; they must have let some of their friends get on, against the rules – no, worse: they accepted bribes from last-minute passengers. I start writing a vitriolic and threatening letter in my head to the head of Air France: the flight attendants will be hauled up before my tribunal. But I daren't formulate my verdict, and I'm ashamed when I guess what it will be, because while I want the two unspeakable flight attendants to be punished, I don't want two young women – unfortunately, the same two – to lose their jobs. I also imagine scathing articles in *Le Monde* and *Le Nouvel Observateur*. The manager of Air France, reading the newspapers, cries: "If only I'd known!" Too late! Air France planes fly empty from now on. Passengers turn away from them in disgust. The Company manager comes to me begging on bended knee. Through his sobs, I hear the words "for the sake of France." This worries me. Do I have the right to ruin the national airline?

As soon as my fantasies of revenge begin to take concrete shape, I'm aware that they're grotesque, and I turn them into silly stories to amuse myself. But that doesn't calm me down enough to let me forget my frustration. The progress of my vengeful fury, disintegrating beneath my awareness of how ridiculous it is, can't seem to achieve catharsis, and it's as if an atmospheric depression were hollowing a place for itself again and again without being able to bring on the storm. So, throughout the day, the vapors of fantasy disperse and reform.

Next day, my thirst for retribution has stopped raging, and has turned into optimism instead. I imagine the head of Air France answering my letter, and offering us, as compensation, a free round-the-world trip in first class.

A few days later, this business is still on my mind, and I imagine a letter signed by the Nobel Prize winners associated with the Salk Institute, indignantly protesting to Air France about the injury suffered, through me, by the scientific community. (A new fantasy: the head of Air France is arraigned by the body of Nobel Prize winners).

THE JOURNEY

Is it because I was preoccupied by the formalities we had to go through each time we changed planes? By this whole sorry business? I was neither curious nor receptive. I hardly noticed the change of human type at Chicago: the cosmopolitan cargo disperses, and we suddenly find ourselves, at TWA gate 12, in the midst of an American population, with withered, painted old women and hulking, retarded-looking men. Johanne is very uncomfortable, she thinks everyone sees us, a mixed-race couple, as a provocation; from Chicago onward, she will do her best not to speak English, and when she does, she exaggerates her French accent so as not to be taken for a Black American.

In the plane, I sleep, I eat, I read absent-mindedly (Durrell's *Tunc*, I'm still not riveted by it, but then I'm only on page sixty).

Suddenly, while I'm drowsing, it dawns on me: social structure is not a literal copy of biological structure, but repeats it in an incomplete and muffled echo. But if that's true, why are only certain species social (bees, ants, termites, humans)? Humanity is the tangential case. While for bees and ants the hierarchical-structural principle is rigidly imposed, and individuals are like cells constituting a social being, in the case of man there is an ambivalence and a kind of ontological instability: which is the being? The individual or society? A confused feeling which can't manage to find expression, a feeling that I'll have to find a bio-sociological analogy and ask myself some questions about the meaning of this analogy. But perhaps that is exactly what I'll have to think about at the Salk Institute.

After the luggage hunt, suspense, transit from the TWA terminal to the international terminal (where at last we find our bags), then on to the American Airlines terminal; final leg in a four-engined Boeing, which covers the short hop between Los Angeles and San Diego in twenty-five minutes.

San Diego lit up by night. A few skyscrapers; the plane, which is descending lower and lower, heads straight for one of them. It passes to one side, and lands. The airport is in the center of town.

Relief: beautiful Chantal and John are there, providential, welcoming.

PEDESTRIANS

We glide through the night. American cars all move smoothly, with no sensation of bumpiness, because of their super-powerful engines. We catch a glimpse of two cops with helmets on and two youngsters at the edge of the sidewalk. John explains. The police are checking their IDs because they're pedestrians. Everyone's in a car here. The pedestrian is suspect. When I wake up, next day at noon, and stick my nose outside, not a single pedestrian can be seen on Princess Street. That afternoon, trip to La Jolla in Chantal's mini-moke, through streets bordered with villas, palm-trees, oleanders, bougainvillea, and still no pedestrians, cars everywhere, driving at a leisurely pace, never hurrying, stopping at intersections; in short, the successors of the extinct pedestrian. Only in the center do we see people on foot, and then not real pedestrians, but motorists who've had to get out briefly to go and run their errands.

Ghost cars.

FIRST TRIPS TO LA JOLLA

It's beautiful. The low Californian villas, often made of wood, surrounded by flowers, bougainvillea, oranges, and other tropical trees, nearly all appeal to me. The streets wind, up and down. The ocean. Hills. Superabundance, luxuriant growth where it's watered, irrigated, and alongside, where they haven't channeled in water, dry earth, burnt grass, desert. A feeling, like a prophecy, that one day all this will revert to desert.

The beach. Surfers. I'm told the surfer only thinks about surfing. How well I understand him. Better than Christ: gliding on the water, letting oneself be carried along, erect, on the crest of the wave, and then, at the last possible moment, tumbling, collapsing. It's making love with the ocean.

On the beach, a dog digs frantically at the sand around a large stone, until he uncovers it completely. He tries to pull it out with his teeth, whining plaintively, then barking furiously. An incomprehensible spectacle. Seeing our surprise, the dog's master explains:

"In Hawaii, he used to dig up coconuts buried in the sand."

So that's it! The poor beast searched the ground joyfully, then became anxious, upset, and finally furious because the stone didn't turn into a coconut.

I think, as I walk away, "Isn't that the same kind of thing we all do?"

Sea birds. Gulls, cormorants, like fashion models twirling down the catwalk, and those sandpipers which patter at high speed on their spindly legs.

FIRST CONVERSATIONS

We chat about this and that, in the evening over dinner. The Californian West is the culture medium for the America of the future. On one side, a kind of neo-Fascism is developing, on the other the radical anti-establishment activity of the young people is in ferment.

John: "It's a profound and wholesale rejection of the American way of life."

Me: "They haven't yet generated the possibility of another society. They've only been able, here and there, to create a counter-society, a parasitic enemy of society, which is in danger of disintegrating as they grow older or become addicted to narcotics . . . "

"Yes, it's a failure . . . "

"No, however short a time it lasts, it has been lived through, it has existed; just as the first heart transplants, in the short time they survive before being rejected, show that it is possible to live *with a different heart.* It's vital that new ways of living should be tried out."

We talk about the communes, group marriages, here and in Europe. I've just been reading Sitbon's article in *Le Nouvel Observateur* about the communes in Copenhagen. Everywhere, either new problems are replacing the old ones, or the same ones are re-emerging. But still this is an effort to escape from the inadequacy, shortcomings, selfishness, and isolationism of the bourgeois couple, of the bourgeois family.

I learn that La Jolla is a retirement home for ex-admirals and old mummies wrapped in bandages of dollar bills. Seven or eight years ago, the Salk Institute and a campus of the University of California (UCSD) were set up there. Echoes of the political struggles in Berkeley. Our friends are pro-student, read the "free press."

John foresees the emergence of a new society based on a hierarchy of three classes. The first of these is the result of collusion between the military class (emerging during the Second World War, consolidated and extended by the Korean war, then the Vietnam war) and the class of businessmen, managers and technocrats who know how to talk to computers. Beneath them, a vast middle class capable of participating in the gigantic productive and administrative machine. And right at the bottom, an immense underclass whose sole function would be to buy and consume.

Maybe he's right . . . But for my part I see American society as a minefield of internal contradictions, from which tremendous crises could emerge, and these in turn could give rise to a kind of neo-Fascism, within which, in my opinion, racist and nationalistic features, in a word political hysteria, would be at least as important as the new Leviathanesque hierarchy.

Three possible crises:

1. economic; today this seems improbable but is not impossible;
2. internal; the Black problem; they are heading for a struggle between two nations which overlap but are separated by the most divisive factor of them all: skin color;
3. external; the crisis of the whole imperialist system in Latin America.

In this heavenly oasis we calmly discuss such cataclysmic perspectives.

THE BLACKS

It's a white residential oasis, an oasis of racial purity: you don't see any Blacks here, or any Mexicans. Only once do we see two young girls in the street, one of whom is Black.

Johanne: "She's her maid . . . "

Chantal: "No, they're friends . . . "

Me: ??

Johanne senses the presence of segregation everywhere.

In San Diego, the newspapers tell us that the police are coming down hard on the Black Panthers.

Read Ronald Steel's article in the *New York Review of Books* on the Black Panthers.

JOHN HUNT

John: I'm finding out more about him, getting to know him, and now above all *I know his scent.* When a dog has had a good sniff at another dog, he possesses a whole range of information about him, based on a sample of various odors. For me, it's the same and the other way round; now I've got a sample of varied information about John, and so I can immediately sniff out all his human odors. He too belongs to the secret brotherhood of orphans, those who were obliged to feel different, and then to be different . . . His father died when he was seven years old, and he only found out why when he was twenty-one. His mother met a half-Indian man, who had studied at Oxford and Harvard, became an executive, and then quit suddenly one day to go back to his tribe, where he rejected the White way of life. John's mother went with him. The old couple live in the ancient way, sleeping under the stars, on the ground, relieving themselves in the open air. They do this in winter (when it gets down to minus 20 degrees) as well as summer. John empathizes with the young people who take the Indian as their model and reject the White man's lifestyle. (Me too, I empathize with that: why? I love and admire the Indians. I have compassion for them and I feel humble before them).

REBELLION

A distinguished and cultured woman shows us a house. She comes from an old Confederate family. *Her son, who's seventeen, has stopped talking to her!* This fills me with enthusiasm and at the same time scares me a little.

In the *San Diego Door for the Liberation* (free press), there's a violent article against technology. John tells me that the young have discovered the bliss of doing nothing. This is linked to their discovering how absurd it is to devote one's life to techno-bureaucratic work. What a fantastic dissolution of values. What a crucible! That's my second goal here: to see these young people who are generating their own counter-society and living out their unscripted revolution.

LA JOLLA

Woke suddenly in the middle of a dream (Wednesday night) just when John (I can still hear his voice in my ear) was telling me:

"San Diego" (La Jolla, probably) "has everything you need for the good life, but people here don't have a good life."

A fabulous Mediterranean coastline, even more Mediterranean than the real thing, with its perpetually temperate climate, its blue sky, and its gardens, which are constantly irrigated with water brought down from the mountains. And yet there's nothing here of the Mediterranean civilization, no café terraces, no outdoor life, no communication, no *agora* . . . Each little monad lives entrenched in his villa, camouflaged by his patio, and only goes out in his car. I'm impatient for the University semester to begin, to see what campus life is like.

SVETLANA

An article about Svetlana[2] in *Look.* The Minotaur's daughter lives in Princeton, the quiet little University town. Interview: "The West is a free society, where people can do as they like, and express their own opinions. This probably results in disorder, but it's much better than order based on oppression . . . I'd rather live freely in disorder."

I'm one of those people who have a double soul, a double "I," and so is John; we can understand and empathize with the revolt of the West as if it were our own, but we can also understand and empathize with the revolt of the East as if it were our own. That's what Svetlana is expressing in her own way.

She also says: "I'm fed up with them going on about the revolution and Mao."

FREE PRESS

In a nutshell, the free press is the reflection and the mouthpiece of this exuberant movement, which is at once formless and multiform, embraces both psychedelia and politics, sexual topics and mystical ones, seeks to establish its identity in a revolution which is sometimes social and sometimes individual (or both at the same time), and encompasses a range of people from the hippie to the militant campus Leftist.

These newspapers (dailies, bimonthlies, monthlies) have their own distribution channels (street vendors, psychedelic shops), as well as some regular sales outlets. There are two free press papers in San Diego, a few more I think in Los Angeles, and several in the San Francisco Bay area, including the *Berkeley Tribe* and the *Berkeley Barb*. The papers I have read so far include four elements whose particular expression and combination seem strange to a French reader. First of all there is the ferocity of the political element: they are not afraid of insulting Nixon, the "establishment" and the "pigs"[3] nor of glorifying Ho, Che, Mao, and the Panthers. One senses that the Marxist vulgate is already profoundly entrenched within the old American radicalism (and one might ask whether this radicalism is being reborn as a sub-species of "Marxist-Leninism," or if it is disintegrating and being supplanted by the latter).

The theoretical element is, in my view, much richer, with its sketchy syncretism mingling and juxtaposing elements drawn from various sources: the psychedelic experience, the great inner journeys, Far-Eastern vulgates, the Marxist vulgate, and the mixed bag of prophets represented by MacLuhan, Marcuse, Buckminster Fuller, William Burroughs, Timothy Leary, etc. (who are not theoreticians in the socio-political sense of the word, nor thinkers in the academic sense, but truly prophets of an eschatological quest). Something is advancing here, searching; it is tentative, candid, intuitive, a mixture of materialism and mysticism, hedonism and asceticism, and I find it both moving and extremely interesting. I notice many unexpected, remarkable formulations whose echoes resonate long afterward in my mind (like "reality is for a privileged class," of which more later).

There is an erotic element, not only in the articles or themes dealing with sexual liberation, but also expressed in the large proportion of the advertising given over to pornographic films and literature; moreover (especially, it seems, in Los Angeles and the Bay Area) there are a great many personal ads where gays, swinging couples or mere heterosexuals keen to meet others advertise their attributes, their qualities and their tastes.

Lastly, there is the aesthetic element, and here a significant amount of space is often devoted to music (especially that of rock groups). There are quite a number of drawings, caricatures, and satirical cartoons, which are very often excellent.

I find all this very interesting, and not only for its "documentary" value: it's inspiring, exciting. I have the impression that, compared to the French Leftist papers (which are either just pamphlets for hyper-politicized sects, or publications that are half-submerged in the big magazine press), these show both more openness and less complacency. Most of all I feel that people write to *express themselves* in these papers, and not just to provide readers with the usual kitty biscuits or doggy chow.

IN THE FREE PRESS

In the *San Diego Door*: "Protest is our most important product."

In the same paper, I read a cartoon over and over: in it a girl gets liberated, joins the underground, takes part in street demonstrations, becomes a militant, leads the hippie life. Her liberal friends, who had condemned her at first for not getting involved in the "social realities of our times," criticize her once again: "My liberal friends said my new way of life was a negation of a responsible social system. It was ignorant of the mental and economic restrictions in a realistic world." And in the next frame, after thinking about it, she concludes, in an admirable phrase: "Reality is for a privileged class."

An interesting theoretical-self-critical-prescriptive article in the *Berkeley Tribe* of August 22, "Free Berkeley," by Frank Bardake and Tom Hayden.[4] A combination of hippieism and Marxism, an association of views which usually negate each other. They insist on the revolutionary role of the young: "Young people are the least settled and accommodated, and tend to have greater aspirations than the older generation." Youth as the revolutionary avant-garde. (Send this article to Lefort).

Read the *Navajo Times*, the Navajo tribe's paper, published in Window Rock, Arizona. Read the *Berkeley Tribe.*

Must study neo-tribalism.

HOME

It's decided. We're going to rent the beautiful villa by the beach that Johanne likes. We're moving in on Tuesday. Now we just have to find a car.

JONAS SALK

Met Salk at the Hunts' party. I think I had expected this benefactor of humanity, this savior of children, to be bearded like Pasteur. His face surprised me: it was clean-shaven, small, smiling, courteous, vaguely absent: a cocktail-party face, like our own . . .

LIFE

Started reading *Developments in modern biology and their implications for society* (Annual meeting of the Board of Trustees of the Salk Institute, February 13, 1969).

Jacques Monod[5] insists on the fundamental theoretical importance of the discovery of the structural unity, at the cellular and molecular level, of all living things. "Everything that is true of a bacterium may also be true of an elephant," etc. Monod believes that humans will not be able to manipulate their own genes, or modify their own nature through the control of heredity, for a long time yet. But he believes it possible to improve the performance of the brain as early as the fetal and neonatal stages; he suggests methods for raising I.Q.

Presentation by Doctor Lehrman on the hypothalamus (cf. pp. 00, 00, 00): it is the center regulating both instinctive behavior and social interaction.

What are the relationships between microcosm and macrocosm, between cell and organism in the human being, between individual and society? . . .

I don't know why, but I keep thinking about Blaiberg's death.[6] It's incredible! For a year, his entire organism, from the central regulating post right down to the least little cells, fought tirelessly – and with the most astonishing skill – to reject the foreign heart, which had become the element most essential to its own survival. Thus there is a complete absence of connection between the conscious part of man – which knows that this heart is absolutely necessary, and does all it can to retain it, but remains epiphenomenonal – and the government of the corporeal organism which, obeying a different and absolutely impermeable intelligence, battles with the savior as if it were a hereditary enemy.

The only strategy one can deploy to get the foreign and life-saving heart accepted is to wipe out or to dupe the antibodies whose job it is to recognize and eliminate the intruder, which in this case is also the liberator. But *when* will we be able to transmit the first message to the depths of our own bodies, *when* will we be able to begin to communicate with what for each person is the most hermetically sealed, most foreign thing there is: his own being?

All this continues to amaze me, and in the evening, I question Bronowski about these rejection mechanisms. He tells me that rejection is not only carried out under orders from the central command post, but is also automatically activated at the cellular level itself. All the cells are mobilized to reject the foreign body. Each cell, he tells me majestically, is an extraordinarily complex entity, with superior organization, and has the same degree of autonomy as you or I in society. I'm still incredulous, thinking of these millions of cells within me, more than the population of the planet, each with its own life, each constituting a universe . . .

What a fabulous interlocking construction, with millions of living blocks constituting one being, which, along with millions of other beings like itself, constitutes another being, which in turn . . . ?

THE BLACK DEBUTANTES' BALL

Rent a tuxedo. I need one to attend the "Debutantes' Ball" for Blacks and Mexicans. At Bob Kofman's, a boutique specializing in such articles, a dozen bust dummies are wearing different styles. Tailor-made shirts of all kinds are displayed under glass. The shop doesn't look like a second-hand store, but gives an impression of discreet elegance. Two salesmen, or rather rental agents, one short and thin, the other tall and fat. A Jewish-looking Laurel and Hardy. You make your choice by inspecting the display and the catalogue. The fat one measures me (shoulders, waist, height, inseam) while the little one takes care of a very hip Black guy dressed in bright colors. The fat one brings me a tuxedo in my exact size, with a shirt, tie, cufflinks. I try it on in the little dressing room. Chantal writes a check. It's a minimal deposit, and they don't ask for ID. When the tuxedo is returned, two days later, with all its paraphernalia, they won't even check it until the customer leaves. It's all done by gentlemen's agreement.

The Black and Mexican debutantes' ball is held in the evening at the Salk Foundation, which has lent its premises for the occasion. In fact, there are no Mexican girls. Just the Black bourgeoisie, in evening dress. The fathers, most of whom are bald (or shaven-headed?), look very peculiar. It's as if the phlegmatic mask of the American businessman had been superimposed over the face of Uncle Tom, with its heavy load of patience, suffering and experience. Perhaps they're putting on an air of frosty reserve in order to complete their resemblance to very proper White gentlemen, and to look as little as possible like the laughing, exuberant old Negro. But their faces have taken on an indefinable sadness and solemnity in the process. What are they? Wealthy merchants? Entrepreneurs? I have no idea. Their wives are enormous Oriental matrons. They look as if they've walked out of one of those Mediterranean women's quarters where uterine fertility is assessed in proportion to body mass. They're wearing very elaborate evening gowns, and seem to be making an effort to maintain their distant and guarded expressions. The girls are stunning. One of them, a (dyed) redhead, half-naked in a very short evening dress with a plunging neckline, has a fantastically wild feline face. I keep looking at her. She's accompanied by a boyfriend or official fiancé, a young Black wearing a white tuxedo and a Hollywood smile. And then as I look around the room I notice, in a dark tuxedo, transfigured, the young Black I saw at the tuxedo rental place.

A few Whites: two or three clergymen who look pleased to be leading their Black flocks into the blessed pastures of respectability, some old ladies (patronesses or their equivalent?), Salk, Bronowski, John. A good band (of mixed race) is playing. We drink California champagne. Then the ceremony – the rite – commences. A pastor makes a speech, followed by a city councilman; then first a Black man and then a Black woman croon an English-style melody, accompanied by the piano; it sounds terribly old-fashioned, befitting a genteel drawing room. Then it's time for the four debutantes to be introduced. A hostess gives their name, age (16), their ambition (to become a secretary or a social worker), and they make their entrances in turn. Each girl is greeted by her father, who gives her a bouquet of flowers, takes her once around the dance floor, and leads her to a table where the mothers and the escorts are sitting. The daughter curtsies to her mother, gives her the bouquet, and then comes back to stand beside her father. Once the four debutantes have been introduced, the piano strikes up a waltz, and the fathers dance awkwardly with their daughters. Then it's a different tune. The fathers present their daughters to the escorts. A ceremonious dance. The initiation is complete.

I try to distinguish the different kinds of melancholy that are mixed up inside of me. Perhaps there's a little, but a very little, of the melancholy I would feel at a town hall dance. There may also be the sadness of seeing these handsome Blacks stifling all the poetry and real music within them, in order to behave like respectable Whites, denaturing themselves in order to be "nice" people. But mostly there is the sadness of knowing it's all in vain, that not for a minute will it make the Whites recognize them as equals.

And I feel at the same time that it's all already too late; that the final effort of the Black bourgeoisie to whiten themselves culturally will soon be repudiated, disowned, swallowed up in and by the rise of Black nationalism. And I finally work out what I'm feeling, which I'd thought was something close to pity. No, it's not pity, unless it's a tragic kind of pity. It's the feeling that an immense calamity is hovering over all this, a past calamity, a present calamity, and surely a horrifying future calamity.

On the way out, John, who must have been feeling similar things, tells me he feels confused. When he was asked, he did everything he could to offer them a place to hold their ball. But radical friends of his told him he was wrong, that in fact he was favoring the Black bourgeoisie, the status quo, etc. I tell him that, if I had been in his shoes, I would have done what he did. To close the door on this ball would have been a concrete act of segregation, in favor of an abstract principle of anti-segregationism. I also tell him that the richest and most bourgeois of these Blacks is more unfortunate and humiliated than even the poorest of the working-class Whites.

OLD TOWN

On Sunday, visit to the Old Town of San Diego. A few Spanish style adobe houses are nearly two centuries old. The town is celebrating its bicentennial. Here, everything that has been around longer than twenty-five years is old, and the eighteenth century corresponds to what Roman antiquity is for us. The museum: there were Indians here too, naked, beautiful and candid. Their civilization was destroyed by the Spanish first, then the Americans wiped out what was left of it.

Mexican restaurant. Delight in rediscovering tequila, which I water down with lime juice, rolling it over my salty tongue.

HOUSES

I like the fact that American houses are not built to last, to defy time.

ZOO

The Zoo. The biggest in the world. One of the richest in the world. Fabulous expanse of grounds. We pass over it diagonally in the cable car called the Skyfari. Open cars follow one another; in forty minutes they complete a six-mile loop.

We stop in front of the condor's cage. He is alone. To me, he looks utterly depressed, desperate. His weedy neck, bald like a turkey's, supports a haughty beak. At the zoo in Rio, we'd already seen a condor in an even smaller cage. Suddenly, we heard a throbbing sound, like a plane about to take off: it was the condor who had stretched out his wings, beating the air for a few seconds, in order to get up onto a little perch a foot and a half high.

Here we are, Johanne and I, in front of the San Diego condor, thinking about the Rio condor. And now the condor comes towards us, and starts plucking at the wire mesh with his beak, as if he's asking us to let him out. As if he's trying to make us understand that he's not asking for food, but is suffering from being kept prisoner like this, he rubs his sorry-looking neck against the cement ledge in which the wire is set, then he plucks the wire again, then rubs his neck again. We are seized by a feeling of impotence and shame, incapable of making him understand that we cannot do anything for him.

A few years ago, at the Berlin zoo, there was a tropical bird, alone in his cage, who darted towards us. He had picked up a piece of straw from the bottom of his cage, and offered it to me through the wire. I took the straw, and immediately the bird started tugging at the wire, pecking at it furiously, which signified very clearly: "I can't take it any more, help, get me out of here." So I offered the bird another piece of straw, and he threw it down, and went to get me a different straw, pushing it out to me again, and a second time, as soon as he had made his gift, he started rattling the wire like crazy. Is it possible that he offered me a gift so that I would help him? Had he understood that I could understand him, and understand his thirst for freedom? What he couldn't understand is that I couldn't do anything for him.

We are so delighted with all these animals that we forget the zoo is above all a prison.

Only the gigantic aviary is not a prison. It's about one hundred yards high, and maybe two hundred yards long (?); it's on a slope, with a waterfall running through it, and luxuriant vegetation; inside, an unbelievable number of tropical birds squawk, sing and fly. It's a concentrated exotic Eden; we walk through it down a twisting path, discovering new birds in fabulous colors at each step. We must come back to this enchanted place.

Dinner that evening, near the Rancho Santa Fe, surrounded by a forest of conifers and eucalyptus trees, looking down over a valley of orchards in the distance. The house we're in is made from fragments of old Mexican houses, assorted but all authentic. A star from Hollywood's golden age had it built. Inside, again, there is an almost absolute degree of comfort. The owners: an architect and his wife, who inherited millions. They have a multi-colored parrot, whose cheeks or jowls are white but blush pink if you speak to him tenderly. Every morning, in a little fluty voice, the parrot asks for his tortilla. If nothing appears, he demands, in a louder voice, "My tortilla!" And if there is still no response, he starts screaming "MY TORTILLA!"

Scientology: Val's boyfriend already talked to me about it in New York. Find out what it is. Also see the Californian religious sects.

Tuesday, 9 September

COOL HAND LUKE

On Monday night, saw this film with Paul Newman playing the hero. An appalling tragedy, which leaves me feeling even more crushed than *Easy Rider* did. Like the two guys in *Easy Rider*, Luke only wanted to have fun. An implacable mechanism ends up putting him in the killer's sights. Once again, as in a whole series of films beginning with *On the Waterfront*, we're watching a veritable Passion, in which the hero endures humiliation and torture. But here there is no consolation; no redemption is offered to the viewer.

DREAM

On Monday night, I dreamed about Bourdieu: I go and ask him for an explanation of his attitude toward me. It's all very well for him to criticize my ideas, but why this personal animosity? In my dream, he remains surly, malevolent. Of course, I ask for his friendship, which he refuses. This reminds me of dreams in which I am reconciled, friends again with Aragon. The thing I find most difficult to bear is enmity.

AMERICA

Morning: I write some letters. I steal a few sentences for this journal from letters I write to Véro and to Monica:

"They have everything here, except the one thing that would give a meaning to all these things" (but which I can't manage to put into words, for it comes from something deeper than the absence of a lifestyle, the lack of happiness, etc.).

"The best of America (technology, comfort, cleanliness, efficiency, climate) envelops the worst of it."

"American society skims off all the ingenuity from peoples' brains and only leaves them with leftovers of intelligence for their own lives."

Then I realize that I am just repeating all the usual European clichés.

Moving into the house on the Camino del Collado. I keep saying to myself: "Three bathrooms!" Ruth has five TV sets at her place. She lends us one.

Johanne likes the house. Will the house compensate for the environment? Here, the two of us being a couple seems at once monstrous and incredible: a White with a Black, and in one of the nicest White neighborhoods too! So incredible in fact that all the barriers are down, taken by surprise. Clearly, what saves us is the fact that we're not Americans. Johanne speaks conspicuously in French to me when we are in shops, in the street, or in front of other people.

Racism, up to now, has been silent around us, at least within earshot, but the newspapers and the TV discuss it endlessly . . .

Ruth: Immediate complicity with Johanne. She is amazed that Johanne should have moved into this house, in this neighborhood. She's really pleased about it, as if it's a clever trick, as if it's an act of revenge. Her husband, who is a valet in a very wealthy home on the hill, looks at me trustingly. They invite us to dinner, and we ask them to come by whenever they like.

Ruth, speaking to Johanne, lowers her voice when she utters the words "colored people."

Dinner at the elegant *Top of the Cove* restaurant; the waiters are wearing tuxedos and shorts. The fish and seafood are tasteless, entirely neutralized, disinfected, and deodorized by the refrigerator. Here we are, right next to an ocean full of fish, but it doesn't occur to these restaurants to go and buy fresh fish at the market every morning.

The Puligny-Montrachet, however, was wonderful.

Wednesday, 10 September

I've got my car, bought for 350 dollars from a French researcher at the

Institute of Oceonography who's going back home. His wife has a lovely open, spontaneous personality. She and Johanne like each other very much. With great simplicity, she says: "It's a shame I'm leaving, we could have been friends" (and I think to myself that maybe I could have slipped into this friendship too).

The car, a 1960 Chevrolet Impala, a huge luxury tank, already has 84,000 miles on the odometer. I have great difficulty getting used to such easy driving: no clutch pedal, no gears, power steering. I don't know what to do with my left foot, which, in the initial confusion, goes crazy and keeps stomping like a brute on the brake pedal.

WOMEN

Bernat is sarcastic about the women here. But I often find something appealing about them. Of course, I'm not talking about the wrinkled old mummies, all made-up and dressed in pastel colors, that you see in all the places frequented by the wealthy, especially in America. I saw one of these old women at the *Shores* supermarket, wearing a little, glamorous, very low-cut gown, her skin spotted with freckles, but not yet ruined, her hair dyed palest blonde, and done like a young girl's, her eyelashes mascara-ed blue, her face perfectly made-up, and in spite of her very thin lips, her body expressed such a will to incite desire that (to me) something exciting, electric, did in fact emanate from it.

I've also seen some young, very blonde, very beautiful women, of the Scandinavian type, with almost bulging eyes and full, curved, pale mouths.

I'm thinking about the three women who showed us the houses for rent:

- the first one, in tennis gear, was 45 to 50 years old, alert, sporty, with a rugged face, leathery and wrinkled by the sun, but frank and open. Her life? Playing tennis?
- the second, a hideous old bat, all withered, eaten away with greed and fear;
- the third – the young widow – in a long dress, very carefully made up, reminiscent of a praying mantis looking for a male to decapitate. This idea enchants me, and I press her hand a little as we say goodbye.

I also think of J.'s wife, a Californian. She has the eyes of a compulsive liar, a nymphomaniac, lost.

Friday, 12 September

Ruth, the plumber, the gardener, the secretaries, the construction workers. They don't make a fuss, they don't hurry; they do their work without looking like they're working. It's not like in our Mediterranean civilizations where you have to fake effort, while the foreman or the boss watches you suspiciously. For us, you have to pretend to be working hard because you want to camouflage the fact that you're doing as little as possible. Here it's the result that counts, and the wonder is that all these people who look as if they're doing nothing actually do things fast and efficiently.

Telephone conversation with Guerrero Ramos, who's in Los Angeles. Great joy. Here, we tell each other, perhaps the most extraordinary experiment in all the history of humanity is taking place.

Saturday morning, 13 September

From the bay window of our bungalow, we see the surfers passing by; they arrive, leave, meet, converse, each holding his elytron under his arm.

Sunday morning, 14 September

The bell rings. Still half-asleep, I open the door. A guy between 28 and 30, who looks like a door-to-door salesman, accompanied by another, younger man, immediately launches into his patter, and I try to understand what on earth he wants to sell me. I get him to repeat it. He starts again, introduces himself, "I'm Larry," introduces his companion, "Larry too," and here he smiles pointedly to make me understand that it's funny. He brandishes a leaflet at me entitled *True Worship versus the False*, then another tract, *Would you like to understand the Bible*. I vaguely grasp that he's a Jehovah's Witness. He asks me if I read the Bible, if I own a Bible.

"Yes, yes, I do . . . "

But he tells me that among all the interpretations of the Bible, there's only one true one, and that he represents the true one. He announces this to me with such a delighted look on his face that I give him a smile of congratulation. I take his brochures, I put off until later the purchase of the little book entitled *The truth that leads to ETERNAL LIFE* which is "pocket size," and (adds the brochure) "easy to understand, only 25 cents."

The brochure also advises us to devote one hour a week to discussing the Bible:

"*Where*? In the privacy of your own home, or at any other convenient place.

When? At any time convenient to you.

At what cost? Completely free of charge."

Eternal life is the cheapest thing you can buy in this country.

Saw *Under the Banner of the Samurai* yesterday evening, by Iroshi Inagaki, starring the great Toshiro Mifune. A color feature, in the Japanese-historical, Western-Shakespearean genre, two and a half hours long. To me, it's an intoxicating cocktail. There are horseback rides and Western-style battles, in fabulous costumes and colors. The hieratic ambience is interrupted by barking dialogue. But above all there is the *narratorial detachment* that I love in Shakespeare's histories or in Boris Godunov. A succession of tableaux through which the destiny of the Samurai Yakomoto, knight errant, precise and ruthless Quixote, runs its course. This "master-less" Samurai can only realize his dreams of grandeur through the intermediary of an overlord, whom he incites to conquer the central part of Japan (the film is set in the sixteenth century, at the height of the feudal period). He makes the man his puppet, manipulating him to serve his own ambition, but at the same time driving the film's plot, which will shatter his hopes and even destroy his love: he persuades the overlord to marry the princess he is in love with himself (in order to save her), and becomes the secret father of the child born to this couple, a child he will support henceforth in its claim to the succession. And all this is achieved through a series of ruses, political crimes and wars which, after twenty years of patiently accumulated victories, come to an end, at the moment of the last, decisive battle, because of a strategic error that proves to be crucial. The dream of extending the frontier all the way to the sea crumbles, and Yakomoto dies at the end of the battle, riddled with arrows. The film closes with the overlord cursing the dead man who, for twenty years, had given him everything, and had led him from one victory to the next: "You crazy fool!" Nothing remains of this grandiose ambition in the land of Kai, which returns to its former life as a sequestered and peaceful valley.

Monday, 15 September

THE SALK INSTITUTE

Here I am at last in the Salk Institute, breeding-ground of Nobel prize winners, and center of pioneering research in biology.

The Institute is enthroned on a plateau, which plummets to the ocean, between La Jolla and Del Mar, beyond the University, and before the Torrey Pines forest. As you approach it from La Jolla, you realize, once you've passed the campus, that you are leaving the California riviera with its gardens, tropical plants, lawns, and bungalows, but you haven't yet reached the burnt California of grassy hills yellowed by drought and sun; the landscape here is a kind of savanna with brush and tufts of greenery on the rocky, sandy ground.

The Salk Institute stands alone. From the height of this austere Acropolis, you can't see the villas of La Jolla, nor the blooming riviera, only the plain, the grassy dunes, ocean and sky. At first sight, the Institute looks squat, like a blockhouse, with its two concrete wings apparently joined around a sort of inner courtyard. But its aspect changes when you go from East to West and from outside in; each of the buildings is six stories high, but two of these are underground; to the West, the blockhouse gray opens into windows with broad frames of tropical hardwood, and, in sharp angles, arrow slits on the north and south faces through which you can see the immense bay windows of the laboratories, running the length of three stories. Is it a fortified city, a castle, or a monastery dedicated to science, in this grandiose and desolate setting? A Puritan public housing block? This building looks like nothing else but it is reminiscent of a thousand things.

An irrigation channel runs lengthwise through the inner courtyard; the water flows into a little fountain-cum-waterfall, a very sober, almost monastic reminder of the Alcazar gardens. It's a modern patio, a central *agora*, and a terrace overlooking the ocean, all at the same time. Yet it all seems deserted. It's a fabulous science fiction-type feeling. You would think nobody was here, and yet everything is functioning.

How can I put it? Ostensibly, this double parallelepiped of a building conceals its true function, or rather, it seems to conceal it but in reality it expresses what is in itself mysterious and Puritan about the Salk enterprise. And I find out about this when I read the internal documentation. Their goal here is not only to promote the progress of avant-garde biology, nor to develop a metadisciplinary science. Their goal is to help humanity to resolve its fundamental problems. Salk's obsession is the good of humanity. That is what was behind his far-away expression; now that I come to think of it I had seen that expression before on Pierre G.'s face, it's the one worn by visionaries. So here is this funny little Jewish man both exhibiting and concealing a vaguely Messianic expression, and it's all shot through with American Puritanism, US philosophy, and "human values" by the shovelful . . .

Inside the Salk, the laboratories and the offices are on alternate floors. I'm on the fourth. The offices are all done out in wood, as are the corridors: luxury, silence, and unbelievable tranquility. They give me the office which only a week ago was occupied by Jakobson (oh yes . . .). Next door is the office belonging to Jacob Bronowski, the house philosopher, a little man with an extraordinary actor's face: he looks as if he's walked out of a Fritz Lang movie from the silent era. Two secretaries, smiling and discreet. I ask for a typewriter. They immediately wheel in a table with an electric IBM on it, and I begin playing like a child, making a good deal of mistakes, for on these Anglo-Saxon machines the A is where the Q should be and the M takes the place of the N. From time to time, I receive some documents concerning the Institute's activities, meetings, etc. From my window, I can see my own portion of the hills and the sea. On this side, the walls have been arranged in a zigzag, so that each window can neither see nor be seen by any of the others, and has its own protected corridor of view onto the ocean.

On the floor below is the library, where *Le Monde* arrives only three or four days late. Between each floor are the toilets, men's and women's alternately. They are like laboratories, absolutely clean, and nearly always vacant; I haven't seen anybody else there yet. A mailwoman makes ceaseless rounds of the Institute, distributing and collecting the letters deposited in each pigeonhole.

And now I've moved into the blockhouse. After a few days, the feeling of having my own *querencia*, my first habits, gives me all the pleasures of familiarity while still retaining those of strangeness and of being in new surroundings. Everything still seems weird to me today: the *agora*-cum-patio, which is still deserted, the incredible tranquility of my fourth floor, with its two secretaries, Cathy and Lee, and the tea and coffee they bring to my desk. In the permanent silence, which is sometimes modulated by a few soft, purely functional, exchanges of words, you can occasionally hear the celestial hum of the jet planes. My astonishment, profound to begin with, becomes more and more intense. Where on earth am I? What is this world? Where are we going? What is life? Today I suddenly felt depressed, as if I had understood that I would never have an answer to these questions . . .

Quick tour of the laboratories. One of them, Leslie Orgel's, fascinates me: they are working there on the origins of life. I don't dare ask any questions yet.

(The *pensoirs*[7]).

In my office, I've stuck the cartoon that ends with "reality is for a privileged class" on the wall, and I meditate on it. It's true, it is only the rich and the privileged who can enjoy social reality, and they expect others to be "realistic," that is, to accept that they must give up their aspirations and their dreams.

BIOLOGY AND ANTHROPOLOGY

Reading the Salk documents

Life reduced to molecular processes, which are themselves physicochemical: we haven't finished dreaming about this yet.

The species and the individual (*germen* and *soma*, genotype and phenotype) together constitute the unity of life, but each entity lives in its particular time and world. Life is this astonishing duality – and complementarity – a heterogeneity between the generative and the phenomenal . . .

Sociology has effaced, glossed over biological Man. Since organicism was repudiated, a century ago, all the bridges between the *bios* and the *polis* have been cut off, and the *anthropos* has been split in two.

Marx, in his *Economic and Philosophical Manuscripts*, had the sense of dialectics, that is of the unity and the rupture that exists between human history and biological evolution. The former is a continuation of the latter, but by other means, down new paths.

In human societies, we can see the principles and processes of evolution in activity, whereas in the living species they appear frozen to our eyes.

If a pan-biology can shed light on social phenomena, then these phenomena can, in turn, shed light on the biological processes which are currently unobservable (cf. evolution).

Is linguistics the new socio-biological bridge? Are there other axes?

Society is a metabolic system: it lives; but is it a living being?

The social being: metabolic and metabiological.

SOCIOLOGY

Study rudiments, elements, even fragments of societies; study temporary societies. Look again at the question of the elementary function of small groups, beneath and beyond Lewin and Moreno.[8]

INTELLIGENCE

Why, in instinctive behavior, is there an intelligence that is so prodigious and yet so completely shut off?

Man's intelligence seems to spring from a leak in the pipelines of unconscious intelligence.

Up to now, Man has only partially reactivated an intelligence that once organized and created the living beings, including Man himself. Man's intelligence is rediscovering the inventions, processes, techniques and ideas which, two billion years ago, were already responsible for cellular organization.

How has this intelligence been reactivated, in flashes and through individuals, allowing the great technical discoveries to be made? Why do we do nothing but start again in a different way, and rediscover?

Why is it so difficult to arrive at an understanding of what is at work in every one of us?

How is it that there is such a hermetic boundary between the system of our conscious life and that of biological structure, with only occasional breakthroughs, dives taken! . . .

There is an intelligence that precedes us, made us, and is within us. Why is it so completely blind? It to us? We to it? (The permanently active creative source: fantasy).

(Dreaming is our truly cosmic activity).

And affectivity?

We are in the dark.

THE INSURANCE SALESMAN

The insurance salesman (for my car). He doesn't even look at the vehicle, doesn't check anything, trustingly notes my declarations about its age, how many miles it's done, my identity, etc. As he hands me the policy to sign, he just asks me to read carefully some lines which he points out to me. It's a printed declaration in which I state that I am aware that any lie on my part will constitute a very serious offense.

As I am about to leave, the insurance salesman confides to me that he too is European. He is English (but a Catholic), he has lived in India, and in Malaysia, he's been in California for a few years; he has ten children. I ask him if he likes living in California. A curious mixture of negative reactions:

1. There is no discipline in the schools here. Of course, the education crisis is international, but in English schools they still have punishment. There is more corruption by drugs here than elsewhere, because of the proximity of Mexico where dealers go and get their supplies of "narcotics."
2. There is terrible hatred between the races here. In India and Malaysia, his children always had Indian or Malaysian friends. Here, his daughter has a "very nice" Black friend (with a pointed look at Johanne) but people can't understand that.
3. (I prompt him with the answer). People don't know how to enjoy life here.
4. They have only one God here. He gives us a knowing look, takes out his wallet, and hands it to us. Johanne and I shout out the answer as if we're on a TV game show: "It's the dollar!" He looks at us with satisfaction.

And then, I don't know why, Johanne exclaims: "Dollars smell, I sniffed one this afternoon." I get a dollar out and stick it under my nose. Johanne maintains that other currencies don't smell and that only the dollar has an odor. It smells, so she says, of musty pockets, of sweaty hands, in other words of Man in society. Does it smell of Man or stink of capital?

Wednesday, 17 September

On Sunday, we're going to the big "park-in" at Griffith Park in Los Angeles. I'm really excited about it, as if I were going for the first time to take part in a ceremony of my cult, my own religion . . .

Very soon, I can feel it, my exploration of the new civilization will begin: the communes, the tribes, "Armed Love" . . . First Los Angeles, and then Frisco!

JOHN

Dinner last night, just the four of us. Wonderful moments of *hermandad*. We talked about those exact things, the communes, the way of life . . . We share the same image-memories, imprinted viscerally: the image of Tolstoy at Yasnaya Polyana abandoning everything and setting off down the road with his cane; the image of the Indian who has graduated from high-school and two universities, suddenly leaving one day to go back to his tribe and live there according to the customs of his ancestors . . .

He pointed out to me that there's something Russian in the sincerity and the candor of the American youth movement, in its sense of sin and guilt, and its need for redemption, which has a tendency to be Messianic and universalist (all this is over-determined by the role the United States plays in the world). And the meaning of the word *love*, which encompasses the mystical and the physical, a word without contours, without boundaries, dripping and syrupy, but also oceanic and sublime . . .

For instance: on TV, Stevie Wonder, the blind young singer and harmonica player, says something nobody would ever say on a TV show in France: "We are only handicapped if our legs can no longer carry us in the direction of love."

Yes, a new form of Christianity and a new form of communism are preparing to be born; I read in the latest issue of *Le Monde* to arrive here (in the article by Frank Jotterand on the "new American spectacle") what Joe Chalkin says about the *Open Theatre*: "reincarnation here and now." To become reincarnate: in the *hic et nunc*, secular, naturalistic version of the *resurrection of the body*.

Beware: this marvelous appeal to love, and joy, this Messianic heralding of Aquarius, could all very rapidly turn sour and veer into fanatical Puritanism (which Marxist Leninism would fit like a glove), or else dissolve into a frenetic *putanisme*.[9] In the free press, alongside the caustic satire and the untrammeled criticism, there are some truly moronic elements.

MOON DUST

A hundred grams of moon dust have arrived at the University of San Diego.

SAN DIEGO

What's this? . . . On arriving at the airport, I became aware of the warlike stance of some big guys with crewcuts, still wearing their street clothes, but already obviously soldiers, who were lining up waiting for their sergeant. Downtown, you do see a few sailors, but mostly it's the night clubs, the strip-tease shows, the dirty movies and the pornographic bookstores which betray the heavy, animal presence of tens of thousands of young men penned up in ships. You have to pass over the Coronado Bridge, or follow the road along the hill-crest to Point Loma, or else drive down Highway 5 towards the Mexican border, to get a perspective on the gigantic basin which is the world's foremost war port, and is in fact currently working for a war, the one in Vietnam; an unbelievable number of ships of all sizes, all steel gray, all with curious turrets, and the skeletal aspect characteristic of warships, are scattered over water which at certain times of day itself becomes gray and glaring.

Although it covers enormous areas of land, the naval base is sealed off, closed to the public, and therefore practically invisible. Thus, one often and easily forgets the very thing that constitutes San Diego's "brand image": the naval war fleet.

On the other hand, as you drive from La Jolla towards downtown, either by the freeway or along the coast on Mission Boulevard, you sense very strongly, all the time, that this is a holiday resort, a place for weekends, for relaxation: there's the row of motels with their papier-mâché decor and their utilitarian comfort along Pacific Beach, and the sailing boats and the little yachts crowding the bay, whose aquatic pseudopodia stretch into the land. It's the American Eden, with the most beautiful sky, the most beautiful sun, the most beautiful ocean in the world . . . The zoo, and Sea World, the kingdom of Sabu the clever, childlike, playful whale, make up an integral, almost natural part of this Eden . . .

The San Diego of honeymoons and holidays, and the San Diego of the US Navy, are only the maritime faces of a gigantic urban protoplasm. San Diego is also the name of a vast urban sprawl, an area without density, at first glance formless, and without pedestrian life, because life there is led only in cars or homes, which means the place is apparently lifeless. You have to leave the freeways, slow down, and look hard to notice that this urban surface, which all looks the same, breaks down in fact into a Black town, a Mexican town, with ethnic neighborhoods, freak neighborhoods, luxury neighborhoods, hippie slums, etc.

There is a center, a little downtown where a few skyscrapers have sprung up in the last four or five years. But this center, in which some pedestrians at last appear, is very strange. You don't see the elegant cream of society there, but the dregs. Here, on Broadway and especially in Horton Plaza, Blacks, Mexicans, old people, dreamers, lost souls, junkies, the unlucky and the mad are hanging around. The center of town has become the dejected, down-at-heel realm of the carless. This is because a new and absolutely different structure has already victoriously superimposed itself over the traditional structure of the town, which is constituted by a periphery surrounding a dense central kernel. This new structure, which is polycentric and automobilistic, is defined by the intersection of four or five freeways, which traverse the urban area, and constitute a circular and circulating network. Shopping centers have been built, are expanding, are being created at the crossroads and the freeway exits. And it is these centers with their gigantic parking lots that are frequented by the shoppers and the consumers, the window-shoppers and the slobbering oglers, the pretty women and the hideous old crones, the middle classes and the wealthy bourgeoisie.

Thus, the true center of the town is circulatory, rotating, whirling: it's the traffic on the freeways numbered 5, 8, 395 and 94, which together make up a huge pump that sucks life in and holds it in check, snatching it up and spitting it out over a radius of fifty kilometers.

THE ITALIAN GROCERY

On Saturday afternoon, we drove around the streets without seeing a single pedestrian. And suddenly, in front of an Italian grocery, the most melodious sound that you could have dreamed of hearing in this deserted urban landscape rang out: *a child bawling.*

The disorderliness of the Italian grocery is an oasis in this geometric desert.

ADOPTION, ADAPTATION

I am adapting to this comfortable life. After three days, everything seems natural to me, the big house with its three bathrooms and its two patios, my Chevrolet tank, the ocean on the other side of the pavement.

THE TEEN-AGER

This morning, at about eight thirty, the doorbell rings; I put a towel around my waist and go to open the door to a girl of about 15 or 16, who repeats an incomprehensible phrase, with an air of conviction. I make her start again. Aha! Rest room, Toilet room. I lead her to the bathroom. Johanne is worried, tells me it's suspicious. She immediately starts fantasizing that a gang of juvenile delinquents have sent this kid on a mission to case the joint. As for me, I fantasize that the kid is taking a syringe out of her bag with trembling hands: she injects herself with a convulsive little moan. We hear the flush; the girl leaves. I stand on guard at the window. It's raining; she's wearing a mini-dress; she hesitates, seems to have decided to head for La Jolla Shores Boulevard, but then sets off in the other direction towards the beach; she goes down the steep path and disappears. Three quarters of an hour later I see her passing by, from my window, with a group of boys and girls, and we wave to each other, and the girl she's talking to smiles at me. So she really did just need to go to the bathroom? That's also possible, in California.

BARKING

On leaving the Salk, I walk past the group of huts which are apparently still used as labs; near the outside wall, I hear a strange noise: someone sawing wood, or a dog in pain?

RESURRECTION OF THE HUMANITIES

Here, I am told, young scientists are abandoning their disciplines, and taking up literature and philosophy instead. O revenge of life against desiccating specialization, against the loss of being!

OLD HO

The *Berkeley Tribe*'s funereal front page in honor of Ho Chi Min. The article represents him as another Washington, an ecumenical Lincoln, a true liberal father and great emancipator. It is in accordance with the models of American idealism that Marxism is becoming the new faith.

Thursday, 18 September

Passing by the huts, this morning, I heard barking, so it was a dog in pain yesterday.

(These scientists butcher their animals, inject them with poisons and horrific diseases, as serenely as the SS doctors at Auschwitz experimented on human guinea pigs).

(The ethical barrier between Man and animals must come down; will it be done by extending to animals the protective principles that Man enjoys, or by removing this protection from Man?)

PSYCHOANALYSIS

Jack Baillet, in an appendix to *Psychanalyse, science et politique*, quotes an article by Shashi K. Pande, "The mystique of western psychotherapy, an eastern interpretation" (*Journal of Nervous and Mental Disease* 146, June 1968, pp. 425–432). The theory is that the analytic relationship simply ends up filling certain gaps in our civilization. The intimate nature of the psychotherapeutic contact, the aura that surrounds it, and the activities that go on without the apparent intervention or judgment of the therapist, all enable a transaction between two people whose acknowledged goal is health and objectivity, but whose hidden goals are quite different. Pande cites a few of them: psychotherapy is a form of love, it is a more or less concealed traffic of influence, it is an attempt to integrate childhood into adult life, it effectively constitutes a critique of the prevalent life style, it tends to free the ego from its alienation and its isolation. These unexpressed needs are related to the particular conditions prevailing in Western civilization: the fact that we attach more importance to work rather than communication and love, independence and personal judgment rather than interdependence and the acceptance of advice from others, the encapsulated individual consciousness, without links to the social and the cosmic, a cerebral approach to existential conflicts.

JACQUES MONOD

I am rereading his inaugural lecture at the Collège de France here, in an entirely new light. What struck me the first time was his recognition of the conjunction of Puritanism and nihilism in an ethics of knowledge. But this knowledge in no way helps promote greater understanding; on the contrary: "Each of science's conquests is a victory for absurdity" (MacGregor).

What interests me today is his theory of life: "There are living systems, there is no living matter." "Extracted and isolated from a living being, there is no substance, nor molecule, that possesses by itself the paradoxical properties (emergence and teleonomy) which are properties of the system, and not of the substances that constitute it."

If this is so, and without lapsing into the Teilhardism[10] that Monod fiercely contests, we can postulate the existence of other systems (living ones?), endowed with different properties, which, although constituted of physico-chemical substances, would be invisible in them. Man might be one of them.

(What he says about the microcosmic cell is fabulous: in the simplest living system we know of, the bacterial cell, metabolism in the strict sense of the term, which is to say the sum of operations ensuring the mobilization of chemical potential and the synthesis of essential cellular constituents, includes more than two thousand covalent reactions, which are distinct and stereo-specific).

(And also: "A transmissible idea constitutes an autonomous entity . . . in itself endowed with emergence and teleonomy, and capable of preserving itself, of developing and of gaining in complexity." Yes, we can and must draw up a natural history of ideas, which, instead of reducing them to their conditions of formation and development, would be commensurate with their own "life." In a sense, idealism quite legitimately recognized that ideas are entities (but by wrongly opposing their kind of reality to material reality). Materialism simply omitted to include ideas among material entities.

THE GREAT CROSSROADS

With this text, we are at the crossroads where two directions intersect:

1. *A general systemology* underlying physics-chemistry-biology-anthropology.

We can already envisage:

a) a physico-chemico-biological systemology (systems peculiar to physical beings);

b) a bio-socio-anthropological systemology (systems peculiar to living beings);

c) a systemology that is applicable to organizations (biotic and social ones) of all kinds . . .

Of course, the problem is how to link up these systems. And to start with, a huge gulf remains, not only between the biological and the anthropological, but also between the physical and the biological. Indeed, based on a physico-chemical system, how can we account for emergence (the property of reproducing and multiplying highly complex organized structures, and permitting the evolving creation of increasingly complex structures) and for teleonomy? (Explore systems theory).

2. *A history of the world*. Here systemology is inadequate, or rather it is as incapable of encompassing the History of the world as the latter is of encompassing systemology. The world, which is a system, is also an event. Observational astronomy is increasingly convinced that the world is the result of an originating, unique, and extraordinary accident. The cosmos began with an explosion, we don't know of what kind, and it will end in a dispersion about which we know nothing. Perhaps it already existed previously, but differently; perhaps it will begin again afterwards, but differently. The world is History, which means: *a*) *a succession of events*, *b*) a bundle of processes, with collisions and explosions, *c*) progression, that is to say, a series of metamorphoses of the first entity (hydrogen or radiance), bringing about the differentiation of the elements and the development of the galaxies.

Life is an organizing system, but it is also a historical fact. The emergence of life on our planet very probably constituted a *unique event*. Evolution is indeed an auto-development of the biotic system, but this development is inseparable from *chance conditions (mutations and natural selections) and from innumerable creations or innovations* (like sexual reproduction, the brain, paws, wings, the vertebral system . . .).

Thus, a science of the world, a science of life, a science of Man, and especially an anthropo-bio-cosmology must be capable of accounting for:

- the system (or the structure);
- the event;
- innovation or creativity.

THE EVENT AND CREATIVITY

The event: a vital phrase from Monod: "All events are improbable." This improbability is related to the absolutely concrete, real and accidental nature of the world.

Everything that has happened in the world, including the happening of the world itself, everything that has been new, or vital – a collision of galaxies, the explosion of a supernova, the appearance of living beings – was all highly improbable. The more important, the more decisive the event, the more improbable it was by nature. "Insofar as a statistical process has a direction, it is a movement towards the mean – *and that is exactly what evolution is not*" (J. Bronowski). Thus, everything that belongs to the domain of anthropo-cosmology has both an event-face and a system-face.

The event is improbability *actualized*. What is actualization? (research, and later do the spadework on the notion of the *actual* according to the microphysical premise and Lupasco's theory).

CREATIVITY

Creativity: it seems that at each stage in the history of life, in each detail of its organization, a *genius*[11] has been at work.

The problem lies in this genius, or geniuses, which we can call invention, imagination, and creation, but which we cannot explain . . .

The gene (in which the information that will govern the construction of the organism's prodigious machinery is contained) is genius preserved. The genius is active in our dreams and our fantasies, but it is unreachable. This imaginative-combinatory-organizational genius is the great mystery; however, although we cannot elucidate it, nor explain it, we can recognize its presence.

What is the link between this genius and chance?

Genius operates in the event, which means the improbable and the accidental: that is, in (and depending on) *chance* conditions. Chance (*improbability and accident*) is omnipresent in the history of the world. The biologists therefore consider it the *operator* (or even the *deus ex machina*) when it is in fact only the *premise* and the agent. The operator is genius, but genius is nothing without the *event* (or, of course, without a *system*).

(Isn't there a factor of improbability, a structural factor, an ingenious factor at work every time progress is made?)

Randomness is one of the twentieth century's fundamental notions. Although repressed by sociologists, it is central to biology (the origin of life, mutations, and therefore evolution), and central to microphysics. It is central to the new arts: the surrealist notion of objective chance, happenings and collages of all kinds, improvisation, parties, celebrations of free jazz or acid rock, etc. *And this is quite understandable*: it is through the encounter with chance that the modern artist works at arousing and awakening *genius* – the same genius which is at work in biotic invention. *The encounter with chance is the encounter with genius*!

At dinner, Johanne says (about a way of cooking carrots, invented in the absence of water, the result of which is delicious): "The lack made the discovery happen."

It seems to me that I'm coming to grips with a key problem: couldn't we define life as an event-driven[12] system, by which I mean a system with a propensity to defend itself and develop in accordance with the external event and the inner event; couldn't we also define life as a random system, that is to say, one that integrates randomness within its very functioning, in order to respond to external hazards?

Life is the only structure that is flexible and responsive with regard to the event and to chance, because it has integrated them both within itself, and that is why life always has two faces: risk and chance.

Friday, 19 September

This morning, while I was writing up the last part of my notes on Monod, I had a feeling of bliss. I felt as if I'd been taken back to my happy days of meditation, on the shores of the Mediterranean, where, cut off from everything, I let my mind focus on what was really important to me. Here, thanks to John, Monod and Salk, I am cut off once again, in this quasi-Mediterranean oasis, invited to think about what interests me more than anything in the world, and at the same time here I am in the place where what matters most in the world to me is in the process of fermentation; I am sheltered, fed, provided for like a pig in clover, precisely so that I can be restored to myself and open myself to the world. This happiness surges up in me so suddenly, so violently, that it is rapidly followed by uneasiness . . . I feel guilty that I am free, that I am doing what interests me, and that this should be granted me as a gift. I have not paid for this happiness, neither with an illness nor a sacrifice . . . At least not yet (??) . . . I'm worried: everything is going too well. Oriental superstition (you have to watch out when everything's going too well); anxiety with which my sense of guilt is mingled, the one arousing the other.

THE NEW AMERICAN SHOW

Read this sentence from Brakhage, author of underground films, including *Making Love*, in Frank Jotterand's series of articles (in *Le Monde*): "From now on, I'm going to devote myself to the unexplored domain of love." He lives in a ghost town in Colorado . . .

"We all know how to change the world, but how will we change the grocer on the corner of our street?"

The Rockefeller and Ford Foundations subsidize the theatre of dissent. Ford subsidizes the black theatre in Harlem where actors preach the extermination of the white race. Dialectic of integration and excessive dissent.

Look for the *San Francisco Mime Troupe*.

TV

Last night, watched five consecutive hours of television. *Tom Jones Show*, *Dean Martin Show* and one or two other shows. The night before I'd already watched the *Dionne Warwick Show*.

Nothing grates, or drags in these shows, they're never boring . . . It's very conscientious, talented work (rehearsed, etc.) combined with spontaneity of an inspired kind, rather than the drivel you see on French TV. There's no strain in the pure, full voices of Dionne Warwick and Eartha Kitt. Moments of adoration when these gorgeous Black chicks appear on the screen. A moment of euphoria where everything is joyous, apparently natural, borne aloft by such effortless talent.

PUNS

The American working class has remained very plebeian beneath the yoke of bourgeois civilization, and at the same time very childlike beneath the phlegmatic mask of adulthood. Hence their still immense, indeed boundless delight in puns. Only the French love word play as much. The American culture industry has selected the neurons into which it pumps pun upon pun, pouring them forth in endless streams on the TV shows . . . Unfortunately, I can hardly understand any of it, but on seeing the audience doubled over with laughter, I start chuckling myself through trust and contagion.

THE THIRTIES

During the years between 1930 and 1940, a polarized situation emerged, with three terms: Fascism, Communism, and democracy. Each of these terms rejected the other two, but also called on the alliance of one of them against the third. Thus, there was an attempt at a democratic-Communist entente (the USSR's entry into the League of Nations, the pact between Laval and Stalin, the Popular Fronts), an attempt at a democratic-Fascist entente (Munich) and an attempt at a Fascist-Communist entente (the Germano-Soviet pact).

Moreover, each of these terms was ambivalent. One of democracy's faces was "freedom" but the other was "capitalism," one of Communism's faces was equality, but the other was totalitarianism. Fascism itself combined the face of chauvinist "totalitarianism" with that of national revival.

Now, the entire political thinking of the time, including – especially –

that of the intellectuals, attempted both to conceal the ambivalence inherent in each notion and to mask the trinal play beneath a binary figure, so that Manichaean alternatives could be proposed purely and simply. For some this meant the alternative between liberty and totalitarianism (Communism and Fascism being identified as two variants of the same system). For others it was the alternative between Communism and capitalism (bourgeois democracy and Fascism were identified as being two variants of capitalism). For the third group it was the alternative between Fascism and Judeo-Bolshevism (democracy and Communism were identified as two variants of Jewish power).

And now, I understand that politics will never make any progress until it gets away from thinking in alternatives (this is what happens when, having examined the ambiguities of a situation, one chooses to treat them as alternatives) and Manichaean binarism (when in fact there are rarely only two terms in conflict) . . . But this is very difficult; it not only involves getting beyond simplification or "passion," but also demands that we contradict the elementary structural rules that govern our thinking. What we need is a form of thinking that remains permanently active, ceaselessly overcoming the gravitational pull of binary/oppositional thinking; we need permanent genius to liberate us from one-track thinking. Can we contemplate making the revolution, in order to liberate genius, until we have first removed its mental chains?

RANDOMNESS AND SCALE

I had noted, from Roger Shattuck's letter to Bronowski: "Randomness and scale, fundamental ideas of the twentieth century, both in the humanities and in the sciences."

As I copy it out again, I try to retrieve the flash that I had found illuminating. For this is what is curious, on reading or hearing certain phrases: the flash that they project. It's a little electric shock, which incites us to destructure or restructure our ideas. A mind that is not receptive to these illuminations from the thinking of others is dead (dogmatic).

We must be capable of being electrified, illuminated. We must be willing to stake our system of the world in the *Game* that is our experience in the world, rather than preserving, consecrating or venerating this system in a Temple-Mausoleum.

NERVOUS SYSTEM

I read in a text by D. S. Lehrman that the nervous system is not only influenced chemically by the secretions of the endocrine glands, but that, in return, it also regulates the activities of the endocrine system, under the effect of external stimuli and psychological influences.

THE HUMAN BODY

"We know for certain that each cell in every organism contains all the information necessary for the construction of an entire organ, and even of the whole organism of which it is a part."

The loss of the capacity for self-regeneration in the specialized cells – *which are nonetheless endowed with the knowledge required for this regeneration* – is therefore the price we pay for specialization. The repressors linked to this specialization have become inflexible and blind. There is a curious deficiency in this ingenious system, which is a result of the inflexibility of the repressive mechanism. However, this inflexibility is not a form of stupidity, which is obvious when one considers that the evolved species, which use the sexual system of regeneration, neglect to carry out any repair work on individuals; in the same way, we don't bother to repair a shoe, a television set, or a broken-down car if it is cheaper to acquire a new one; we throw it away. And this is also true for our bodies, our brains . . . for our souls . . .

But humans are no longer willing to accept such a subordination of the individual to the species. We find it hard to accept the fact that we deteriorate physically before we are able to complete our emotional, intellectual and moral development. Human individuals would like to have self-regenerative capacities at their disposal, and these do exist within us, but they are blocked off, double-bolted, locked in a way that remains a mystery to us, hidden in places whose existence we are only beginning to suspect.

The new individual/society/species relationship, which is characteristic of Man, will call for the control and exploitation (by the individual and/or society) of the self-regenerative biological capacities that have been inhibited by a specific form of repression for ten to twenty million centuries.

Humanity will pursue its historical evolution by using science to make its own biological system evolve. This evolution will follow "natural" evolution, and, like the latter, will perform a regressive-progressive leap (a restoration of potential in the non-specialized cells, but going far beyond specialization).

REPRESSION

The biological "repressor" reactivates thinking about social repression, understood not only as oppression by power, but also as an aspect of organization. There can be no truly revolutionary thought without a general rethinking of the *organizational-repressive system* inherent in life and society.

Now, if we eliminate oppression (pertaining to class, ethnic group, race) and "over-repression" (where the organizational system submits to the sclerosis of the repressive system) from the theoretical field, we come to a key problem: that of *the tragedy of organization.*

In fact, even when it is "functional," repression always, in one way or another, attacks the *generative* (productive, reproductive or creative) forces; and it does so within the specialized cell as well as in society (where ideas, dreams, and desires are repressed). The tragedy of organization is the antagonism between repression and creativity, both of which are necessary to it. *Repression always strikes blindly at creativity. If creativity were completely liberated it would destroy organization.*

The problem is, how can we reach a superior level of organization, which means, how can we implement the thorough reform of the organizational system, which means, how can we establish a new relationship between repression and creativity?

In any case, we must approach the problem of organization/repression in a revolutionary fashion, both at the level of the human organism, where the development of the individual has recreated the need for somatic self-regeneration, and at the level of social organization, where we are still at the primitively experimental stage.

DEATH

Some biologists think that cells contain a precise self-destruct mechanism, which, at a given moment, brings on senescence and death. Thus, they say, the death of individuals is not only or not so much inscribed in the order of life (wear, damage, decay); it is actually preprogrammed. It's as if the phylum were wary of the soma, as if the species were wary of the individual, and so had deliberately set an ineluctable time bomb in the first gene which was programmed to blow up the organism.

How horrible! All this will have to be changed!

ECSTASY

What does this word signify, biologically? Does the cell experience ecstasy?

LOVE

Toward an ever greater dissociation between the act of love and the act of procreation. The act of love is increasingly becoming an ecstatic act.

WHALES

A few sublime seconds in a tedious documentary about whales. We look down, from a helicopter, on a transparent ocean flecked with sunlight, where two loving and joyful whales, bleached white by the sun, are diving, cavorting, and exchanging long caresses, rubbing their whole bodies together. It's a fabulous dance of love, in the "sea mingled with the sun." What's more, the jerks and twists of the helicopter and the bewildering rapidity of the whales' movements, which have forced the cameraman to keep re-framing his shot, in a series of brusque jolts, render the picture all the more juddering and unsteady. And once again I thought: these images are beautiful because they are imperfect, unsteady, ungainly; they are beautiful because they tremble like me and because I tremble like them, in our search for and grasp of the marvelous, the unique and the fugitive.

Tuesday, 23 September

IMPATIENCE

I feel all agitated at being so calm, at not having a set deadline for handing in a particular piece of work. I am already impatient to start writing some suggestions for the Salk, or a text on "science and ethics." I wait fretfully for letters . . . I have to struggle against my impatience. Can't I live calmly? Will this always be denied me? I have at my side the exquisite, divine being of whom I have always dreamed, who is mentally and physically everything that I love, and still I can't be happy? Can't be satisfied with that? Is it my organism that can't bear this excess of happiness, this continuous plenitude? Why has my desire taken refuge in dreams at the moment? Why these fantasies elsewhere? Miserable idiot that I am, will I destroy my life?

Black whirlwinds of my madness, I feel them close to my surface.

I have always wanted contradictory things *together*.

Why have I hurried all my life? Was it to elude my natural torpor? Without all this hurrying, assigning myself deadlines (such and such a date for handing in a manuscript, etc.), I would not have been able to achieve anything . . . But isn't it also making me hurry to do what I have to do, as if death were pursuing me? Is it also because I gave myself too many things to do, always incapable of prioritizing and disciplining my curiosity? . . .

CALIFORNIA HOUSES

These low houses, on hills or cliffs, are to my mind the perfect houses. They represent the synthesis of the ancient Roman house (with its single story), the Spanish-Arab house turned inward on its flower-decked patios, the extraverted glass house opening outward onto the landscape, and the ultra-modern style with its geometric lines; the predominant material is wood, archaic and warm. Wood on the outside, wooden walls inside.

Neo-archaism: some homes attain the height of luxury in their extreme return to rusticity; the living room becomes like a great barn, without a ceiling, under open beams, and is separated from the kitchen by internal walls about six feet high. The house has returned to its primordial nature, so that it's really a *roof*. A magnificent tree grows in the living room at the Orgels' house. It was there when they were building, and they left it.

A very nice couple, very intelligent. Very pleasant evening; the French wine is exquisite, the beef succulent; after the meal, Johanne got us all to dance.

LOVE

When I am senile, which means when I no longer have my critical defenses, I will found a religion (of love): that's what I was contemplating, euphorically, during the dinner at the Orgels'.

And I was also musing, while thinking about the Carcasonne letters, and remembering my "Why do we write?" in *Le Vif du sujet*;[13] in fact I don't only write to express myself, communicate, give, receive . . . and I made the startling discovery that I also write to be loved in the exact way that the woman who had read me with her whole being loved me.

WAITING (AGAIN)

Desperate need to write letters (and also the fun of dictating letters in English for friends). Impatient wait for the mail. I like disconnection, as long as I remain connected.

THE INCULTE OF PERSONALITY[14]

I'm reading an article in *Le Nouvel Observateur* on Ho Chi Min: "He was loved. Vietnamese Communists do not practice personality cults. His portrait was everywhere . . . "

Stupefaction interrupts my reading. What? I go on:

" . . . but it was surrounded by three other portraits . . . "

Phew: so they're only talking about a tetrapersonality cult . . .

From 1940 onwards we frequented the same circles, and almost came into contact, but never met. He thinks he's de-Stalinized, but I see the same old logic ready to spring up in him. For instance, he says to me about J.M.'s thought: "It's very dangerous." On Israel: "It's the most racist state in the world." I hardly have the energy to keep up my side of the conversation.

SCIENCE

The will to monopolize science is characteristic of non-scientific thinking.

"The concept of science is neither absolute nor eternal" (Bronowski).

Science is easy to recognize within its institutional centers: it's what researchers do in laboratories. But how can it be recognized when it is at work outside the official laboratories, in its adventurous forays into the heart of non-science?

LOS ANGELES

Weekend in Los Angeles

On this enormous five-lane highway – ten lanes counting both directions – which crosses a desert of hills, and among this steadily advancing traffic where the cars occasionally pass each other, but do not overtake, I feel like a corpuscle in a blood vessel. This impression is confirmed in the six-lane freeways of Los Angeles, and in its rectilinear avenues and streets.

In Los Angeles, as in San Diego, there are no pedestrians, except at a few points on Hollywood Boulevard and Sunset Boulevard. We are all automobile corpuscles, each following its path with regularity and rectitude . . .

It's a strange bio-cybernetic organism . . .

Everything is on a macro-scale. Even in San Diego, a minor city, the freeways are twice as wide as Parisian highways, and in addition they cross over, making a knot around the heart of the town; the urban area is more extensive than that of Paris, and more airplanes leave from this local airport than from Orly.

Whole sections of Los Angeles resemble stands and pavilions made of cardboard, like the scenery at a world's fair. There are residential suburbs and bare hills within this urban area. No true center, but several nuclei, very far apart from each other. It's the fairly recent skyscrapers in the downtown area which are beginning to define a center. American towns are like that, either an indefinite and infinite surface sprawl, where single-story buildings predominate, or a series of skyscrapers.

The Venice neigborhood (Venezia . . .), south of Santa Monica, by the water. A superb beach, an ocean walkway closed to cars, shops, all of which are kosher, two or three synagogues on the seafront, grim brick houses, very elderly men and women, hippies, young Blacks . . . This Sunday afternoon, after the crowds and the lines of cars this morning and the day before, we make a picnic of freshly boiled (and freshly caught?) crab on the purpose-built picnic tables dotted about the waterfront. Setting sun, calm, peace.

JANIS JOPLIN

Janis Joplin show, at the Hollywood Bowl. A procession of cars, jamming together in a gigantic parking lot, groups of young people wearing the most extraordinary outfits, an open-air amphitheater in which there are maybe twenty or thirty thousand people, and, on the stage, some miniscule insects wriggling about, while music wraps around us. Still, it's disappointing. Not much electricity generated by the first two bands. It starts happening when Janis Joplin plays her opening numbers; at the beginning, her hysteria seems a little forced. But by the end, Janis has warmed up; she braves the deadline imposed by the police, and erupts, screams, swoons. Waves, spasms wash over the huge crowd. It's all over just when it was beginning to get going. Frustration.

PARK-IN

I expected so much from this park-in. Dancing, music, love, fucking, religion, a party, that great party I've been waiting for all my life . . .

The park-in at Griffith Park was announced in the tribal press. A fist closed around a flower, the symbol of Armed Love, summoned us to oppose the proposition which, if it became law, would mean seeking authorization for every meeting held in California's public places with a PA system and crowd control.

Griffith Park is a huge park set on hills northeast of Hollywood. We arrive at about one in the afternoon, and on leaving the freeway we join a procession of cars, moving at walking pace, stopping, setting off again, a gigantic tailback looking for parking garages, all the spaces having been occupied long ago. A stench of fumes. Engines are overheating. These monster cars are not designed for hanging around. First one, then two, then more and more cars are forced to stop, with their engines smoking, radiators dry, hoods up; the procession swerves past them and makes its way incredibly patiently. Not one bus or group coach in the line. These youngsters, the most love-starved on earth, are also the world's richest kids. Still, distances are so vast in Los Angeles that a car is as indispensable as a space capsule to get you from one planet to the next. All kinds of cars, all kinds of young people, Whites, Mexicans, Blacks, all dressed in their own way, but all wanting to show that they are *different*. The procession snakes, goes uphill, down, it's never-ending, stifling, my temperature gauge tells me that my engine's getting dangerously hot. The procession files out into the huge field where the park-in is being held. From a distance we can see a massive gathering. Policemen are directing the traffic, and send us away from the promised land. Finally, along with a few others, I park in a place where it's strictly forbidden, alongside the sidewalk; I leave my hood up to make it look like a breakdown.

We leave the procession of cars, which stretches out into the distance, and join the pedestrian procession headed for the gathering. The same astonishing sartorial anarchy we saw at the Janis Joplin show predominates; there's only one rule: don't wear anything which resembles, closely or remotely, a gentleman's suit, or a lady's dress. It's partly a desire for disguise, but mainly for transfiguration: they want to resemble non-industrial humanity, at least externally to begin with. Indian costume is being modeled in the first row: jacket and/or trousers of braided leather, with long fringes, and a ribbon round the brow. There are also eighteenth-century or Romantic outfits. This jumbled stream of costumes from other times and other places advances; the faces look simultaneously serious, distant and candid. These are not the grinning faces of people who intend to have a good time, nor the solemn faces of those preparing to celebrate a rite. Has American unemotionalism already set in? No, they look to me as if some inescapable necessity has possessed them, and is pushing them forward, and I find this striking and moving.

The park-in resembles both a picnic and a ceremony. The crowd sitting on the grass fills a circle. At a point on the circumference, and not in the center of the circle, there is a group up on a podium, some trestle tables, a sound truck, and another truck on which two long-haired youngsters dressed as eighteenth-century courtiers are dancing, intoxicated. In the crowd, here and there, a few more are wiggling and writhing to the beat of the band. Outside the circus filled with human matter, little satellite groups are scattered about; here couples embracing, resting together; there, "family" groups, with little half-naked children. I come across a table covered with Trotskyist literature, including a pamphlet by Ernest Mandel indicating the paths to an American revolution. A Black man dressed as a Buddhist monk, with a shaven head and a little tuft-like bun, offers me a mystical journal, which I accept; I also gather some Scientology brochures, including the *Study of Truth*, with this motto from Einstein: "eighty per cent of the brain is never used." Various bearded men are brandishing the Bible in the name of their particular sect. A group is seated in a circle around a bearded, long-haired guru who looks like Rabindranath Tagore, they're murmuring in unison the sacred syllable OM. Motorcycles, classic models as well as *Easy Rider* choppers, are lined up together, and nearby are their drivers, real angels from hell, terrifying and fascinating to behold. Each gang-member has the clan name emblazoned on the back of his leather jacket, which not one of them takes off, despite the heat. One of these names, *XIII Dynasty*, strikes me with its implacable, ancient beauty. A remarkable couple comes up beside me while I'm listening to and watching the band from behind. The man is bare-chested; they've smeared each other's face and body with blackish mud, the worst kind of filthy city mud; they're huddled together, and their eyes are wild; he's shuddering, almost trembling, with a strange smile on his half-open mouth, in a state which resembles both high fever and ecstasy . . . They must be on an LSD trip. Nobody looks at them. On the periphery of the circle, the pigs, in groups of three, are maintaining surveillance, looking out for marijuana, which is being smoked openly inside the circle.

One has the impression that a great religion is struggling to emerge, as in the first two centuries AD, when the cults and mysteries of Mithras,

Osiris, Cybele, and Jesus, among others, were multiplying and competing with each other. Here, innumerable sects all aspire to become the main religion: Buddhists, Trotskyists, Maoists, pacifists, Bible-bashers, Christ-lovers, Scientologists. It's religion, even more than God, that they are seeking – a religion which will unite humans with each other and with the world. What will they worship? *Love*! *Love*! The word is repeated everywhere, this word that sounds obscene to French ears the minute it extends beyond the loving couple. Here they say it with simplicity, insistence, innocence and ardor. *Love*, *Love*! We wander slowly, John, Allen the student and I, through the crowd, this flock of love, these unarmed cattle who would be so easily slaughtered, worked on by the ferments of music, revealed religion and revolution. Oh, the lovely faces of some of the young girls! Johanne and I spotted a stunning Mexican woman, who seemed to represent a concentration of all of the Indian, Berber and Spanish types of beauty. Suddenly, the gaze of a young girl sitting on the grass, apparently accompanied by two or three girlfriends, stops me in my tracks. I'd already been sweetly stirred by some lovely smiles, so open, so engaging, in which niceness and desire are undifferentiated to the extent that all the different germinations of love seem possible; the night before I'd been seduced by the smile of a blonde I met at the Ventura party; and now this girl's face is looking into mine and smiling, telling me, without saying a word, absolutely fearlessly, and absolutely without effrontery: "I'd like to know you." I'm so shaken that I lower my eyes, I disconnect, I go back to John and Allen, and, a short while afterwards, since Chantal and Johanne are feeling uncomfortable in the crowd, we leave. I express my regret vociferously. I would have liked to stay in that great mystical corpus, and wait, see, melt into it, sing and dance, or do nothing and sleep. But it's mainly that lost smile I'm nostalgic about, and if I don't go back to the park-in tonight, it's not only because of the hassle of driving at night, in my enormous tank, through the infinite traffic jams, it's not only because I'm afraid that in the end nothing will happen, it's because I know that smile is forever lost to me, and has left for other galaxies.

For twenty-four hours I'm very cross with myself. Through laziness, lack of momentum, lack of courage, I didn't return to the park-in. I find myself back at my lowest ebb.

Thursday, 25 September

I LOVE AMERICA

Until yesterday, I didn't like America. I was fascinated by the country, by the civilization, but I had no form of sympathy for or interest in the people. Over the past few days it has been as if a membrane, a hymen, was quietly and invisibly (to me) beginning to split open. My interest in young people was, until now, un-American, anti-American, in the sense that I sympathized with the existential avant-garde of the international youth movement here, and with American youth in its revolt against the American way of life; but yesterday I began to understand, and now I also like this youth *because* it is American. It must all have started with the smiles of the young girls; then the internal process began to speed up when I became capable of sensing, in "love," the existence of a peculiarly American mysticism. Then, yesterday, there was the seminar on the San Diego Crisis Center, and the hymen suddenly tore last night while I was watching *Midnight Cowboy*. It was in this movie, so full of tenderness, candor and brutality, that I discovered (the profoundly moving aspect of) America.

THE CRISIS CENTER

The day before yesterday, the Salk Institute's weekly seminar was devoted to the Crisis Center. I found the word crisis vaguely attractive, but I was afraid that it was going to be a center for medical diagnosis, whose functions would be explained to us. In fact, as we were told by two of its leaders, a young man and a young woman, it's a militant foundation, whose goal is to provide help in all domains, material, medical, and psychological, for those who have been crushed by society. As soon as I begin to understand what it's all about, I find myself in an indescribably feverish state, everything is buzzing in my head, anthropolitics, militancy, the "foundations." This is in fact, in my view, one of the first foundations in the Asimovian sense of the word. It is allied to the first charitable and militant movements, but surpasses both charitable works in their institutionalized, integrated nature (always set up within the confines of society), and abstract militancy (always shortsighted about concrete individuals). Of course, I'll have to go and see. I've made an appointment on Monday evening, at their place, in the Black ghetto. At the same time, I meet Mang, whose wife is deeply involved in the commune movement, and I set up a meeting for next week, after I get back from New York.

I leave in a state of great excitement, pleased to have established my first contacts with the reality I was looking for, and thinking about what "Foundations" ought to be:

1. Communes: centers of communal life and / or communal work;
2. Mutual assistance and action centers (crisis centers);
3. Centers for research and diagnosis.

Establish more and more workshops of all kinds . . . Promote great ecstatic gatherings . . .

REVOLUTION

Yes, yes, I'd already predicted that the rejection of bourgeois life would come out of the experience of bourgeois life, that the source of the true future revolution was there . . . , but it's still so embryonic, so rudimentary, ill-equipped, lacking the resources to tell the difference between true and false gospels. Already the disintegration of bourgeois society is imminent and still the new society is impossible.

THE SECOND CENTURY

It's the second century of the Roman Empire; the new religions of salvation are multiplying. But this time, it's the great god Pan's turn to be reborn. Who is dying? A vital question which I don't know how to answer. A class? An empire? A civilization? A religion? A world? Our world? Who will be born?

(Historians of the second century should come here to understand the phenomenon of salvation religions in their nascent state. Talk about this to Leroy-Ladurie).

Christianity was eclipsed after the first century, which is to say as soon as people had proof that the end of the world that had been announced to them was not going to happen, and when the Church began to construct itself on a radically different basis from that of the Gospels. *In the same way*, today, Marxism has been eclipsed. Which promises us a sorry state of affairs in the future.

SCIENCE

Austryn Wainhouse tells me that they put some uneducated Black children in the Salk laboratories during the vacation, and that these children made a very valuable contribution to research. Check this, then stick it under the noses of the French sociologists.

PANTHERS

The panthers are in the shadows.

AT WHITE FRONT

It's a giant discount supermarket, selling *everything*. But the cashier bursts out laughing when we ask her for a coffee grinder.

DREAM

Two or three nights ago, I dreamed about Kanapa, just as I had dreamed about Bourdieu a short time before. And once again, I realize that I dream of friendship with people who hate me. This time, I was having a cordial lunch with my adversary, and at one point I reminded him of his past attitude. Clearly, I was just waiting for him to utter a word of apology before falling into his arms. But my adversary pretended not to have heard me. Afterwards, I found myself walking along the street with him, going up the rue de la Montagne-Sainte-Geneviève towards the rue Soufflot. I realized that he was ill, that he was dragging his feet, and I don't remember if I felt pity or pleasure.

(It was Banco who spoke to me about my adversary a few days ago).

YOUNG WOMEN

Letter from the "young women's" association asking me to speak at their congress. I like the name of this association. Yes, young women, associate, unite, and ask what you will of me. It is to you that I address myself, you are the only beings with whom I feel an imperious need to communicate, and what's more, the magnetism you exert over me is increasingly fabulous . . . (This is not the answer I will be sending them . . .)

THE SAW, THE DOG

I hear it twice, three more times when leaving late in the evening, the dog yapping or the sound of a saw, in the medical huts. It makes my blood run cold.

Tuesday, 30 September

WORKING CLASS

On TV: a construction workers' union meeting on Thursday night in Chicago; the workers suddenly set upon some Blacks, unleashing their fury; it's to safeguard their White jobs. I say to myself that such a shocking, violent, scene should make those who believe that the working class is the repository of all revolutionary virtues feel uneasy. But no, they'd just say that the working class is "mystified," which, in their eyes, would explain everything.

VIETNAM

On October 15, it will be national protest day against the Vietnam War.

SALK

We find him increasingly moving. This biologist thinks only of saving humanity from the destruction that biology is preparing for it.

THE NEW HUMANITIES

To build new humanities, a new philosophy, on the foundation of the biological revolution, which is to say on the fact that we are made of amino acids and proteins, now that really would be presumptuous. *But making a new Man, a metanthropos, is a concrete possibility.* Our entire philosophy is collapsing, and yet we can procreate a new being. The real problem, the only non-technical problem, is that of the model of Man, or rather of post-hominid, that we should build. And I agree wholeheartedly with Jonas Salk about this problem. The model must be the concrete realization of humanism, at the very time when humanism is collapsing . . .

READ

Our conception of physics must be entirely re-thought. Yes, but how?

THE PARTY AT JONAS' PLACE

This Argentinean woman, we love her . . .
In these isolated houses, there are creatures like solar systems.
Strong feeling that love can, should, come in a bunch.

ALTERNATIVES

My childlike (childish) revolt against the necessity of choosing (which is to say eliminating) has become my intellectual revolt against alternative thinking.[15] But alternative thinking actually corresponds to the structure of our mental operations, which itself is one level of the binary structure that is so profoundly anchored in all orders of life. This structure is the principle that underlies organization, classification, construction, etc., etc. But I believe that it is responsible for the structural weakness of the mind, which extends far beyond the weakness of the structural mind. Can't we at long last tear ourselves away from these alternatives between intellectualism and existentialism, empiricism and rationalism, objectivity and subjectivity, etc.? Dialectics was and remains the first attempt to go beyond the alternative (and it runs the risk of falling back into confused thinking). It is the effort to tear the alternative away from being a choice between two terms that are indeed contradictory or antagonistic, and to situate this choice between a new formulation and the old one. That's the path to take. My refusal of the alternatives of contemporary thinking (among the intelligentsia) makes me even more of an outsider, and exiles me.

CORRECTIVE ADDENDUM

In fact, positing the alternative is the stock method for getting out of contradictory duality. Nevertheless, everything that is creative in life and in thought has come from something beyond alternatives: *the appearance of a new term, emerging out of the contradictory tension itself.*

Now, what is extraordinary in living structure, and in mental structure, its offshoot, is the coupled system of two antagonistic poles or currents which, whenever faced with an event or a problem, cause a contradiction – that is, two antagonistic possibilities – to emerge. In other words, the same system that leads to the alternative also makes dialectics (the emergence of the third term) possible. Now I understand more clearly the meaning of my refusal to think in alternatives, and my fidelity (in spite of its dangers, but there is no escaping from danger) to dialectics.

SOUND THINKING

A great thinker forges ahead armed with a fixed idea.

A mediocre mind picks up a little bit of everything from everywhere, and ends up with an eclectic mess.

An intelligent man has no fixed ideas and is not eclectic.

NOTES

I'm behind schedule. I've accumulated some notes based on my reading about biology, language, anthropo-biology, and socio-biology.

There are also my notes on the Crisis Center, which we visited last night. This experience made a great impression on Johanne and me.

Put it all off until after I get back from New York . . .

(For the past three days, I've been going to the beach at midday, and I play at diving into the waves as they unfurl. It's intoxicating, it's exhausting . . . That must be why I feel so lacking in energy).

The fog that had covered La Jolla for the past eight days disappeared yesterday. Every pore in my skin is enjoying this blue sky, this sun, this ocean, this landscape . . .

Monday, 6 October

A mass of accumulated notes.

THE CRISIS CENTER (29 September)

The heart of the Black neighborhood. As we get out of the Wainhouse's car, we agree "let's speak French." Over the summer, there have been shootings, homicides, riots, fires, and looting here. We speak loudly in French, but the Blacks stationed on the sidewalk don't seem aware of our presence. A police car is waiting in the shadows; its engine is purring softly. The atmosphere seems tense, heavy with anticipation. As in the jungle, where the animals are all ready to pounce; they pick up each other's scent, but never look at one another.

The Crisis Center is on the first floor of a two-story house, a tin can for humans, like most of the town houses here. A steep, narrow staircase leads to a corridor where a group of adolescents, most of whom are about sixteen or seventeen, are waiting, sitting on chairs or on the floor. The rooms give an impression of untidiness, informality, militancy.

The crisis centers, which are militant foundations providing assistance and solidarity, have been created to meet existing needs. The one in San Diego was founded by students training to be social workers, and they have combined their professional training and their militant aspirations in this enterprise. The center was not designed to provide medical or legal assistance when it was set up: it was the need for these functions that led to their creation, because when sick people came, doctors had to be found for them, and when there were legal problems, they had to find lawyers, etc. Nowadays most of the center's activities turn around these two axes: three days a week are devoted to medical care, and three days to legal assistance. Most of the medical care is dispensed to the young people who live in makeshift communes on the beaches, and whose ailments include overdoses of barbiturates and narcotics, abscesses and infections from syringes (these teenage addicts go looking for used, bent, rusty needles in the hospital trash cans to inject themselves with), venereal diseases, hepatitis (very common among these youngsters who have to rely on whatever food they can find), viruses and infections which circulate in these close-packed human colonies, and premature pregnancies. In the last case, as in that of intoxication, the Crisis Center operates on the margins of the law, and keeps the unfortunate youngsters out of the hands of the police; in ordinary hospitals, they would be interrogated and charged. At the rock concerts, vast open air meetings where people pump themselves full of drugs to their heart's content, the volunteers pick up the kids who are lying stoned out of their minds on the ground, before the "pigs" intervene.

As for the legal assistance section, it deals with evictions, divorces, arrests, and aid to prisoners.

They get their money from private donations, including from some churches; at the concerts, militants from the Crisis Center pass a hat round the audience, who make their contributions out of solidarity. The center is looking for other sources of subsidy: for example, the other night, we sat in on a doctors' meeting, where they were drawing up a questionnaire for research into drug use; the federal budgets that may finance their survey would also allow them to extend medical care to a great many sick people.

We and the Wainhouses are very impressed. For my part, I believe this to be a real "Foundation," whose role is both to counterbalance the harshness of the existing world and to prepare for something new. The simultaneously concrete and principled nature of their undertaking is remarkable: this is not ideological, purely verbal, generalizing militant action, which never actually gets down to the level of concrete individuals, nor is it like the voluntary work of the scout organizations or charitable bodies, which provide for a few poor people while also saving a few souls; elements of all of these things are cross-fertilized here, reconciling Christian charity (*caritas*, the impulse that comes from the heart) with the *caritas* of the secular militant movement, and revolutionary action. In my view, its revolutionary nature can be characterized as follows: the Crisis Center, by extending a solidarity network made up of doctors and lawyers, volunteers and friends, has already begun to create a social fabric unconnected to the circuit of profit; time and services are given up to unpaid and useful activities, and this constitutes, in embryo, the economic and moral fabric of another society within society. In a very concrete fashion, and without initially intending this result, the Crisis Center is helping the communes to survive. From town to town, and from region to region, they could set up networks, linking crisis centers, communes and foundations of all kinds . . . Already, Mang tells me, the switchboards are ready and waiting . . .

There's one thing I find both surprising and worrying, however. Why haven't we seen a single Black in the corridors of this Crisis Center, which is located in the heart of the Black neighborhood? A Black collaborator at the Center suggests that it's because the majority of young Blacks are on welfare, because Blacks seek the services of doctors much less often than Whites, because they have their own solidarity . . . But these explanations are not satisfactory: the very corner on which the Center stands is frequented by dealers selling barbiturates and heroin. Even here, the race barrier is in place; the Blacks are wary . . .

BEACH COMMUNES

We learn that along Ocean Beach and Pacific Beach there are also communities of homeless fifteen-year-olds, gathered together in tents. These fraternities of poverty and love, cold and heat, smoke and inject drugs. The "pigs" will not leave them alone. Since there is a law against living on beaches, solidarity buses go and pick them up, and take them off to spend the whole day on deserted beaches, twenty-five miles away, which are not patrolled by the "pigs". These boys and girls are, we're told, from the middle class. What extraordinary force of rejection could have compelled them to leave their families like this? What horrors lie behind it? What desperate, frantic need for something different? What search for paradise or death?

And I wonder: paradise or death? What fabulous world have they set out to discover, beside the ocean, into what ultraworld have they plunged, under the influence of acid or heroin? What oceanic and placental love are they seeking? They are right to vomit up this world, which thinks about nothing but money, this empty bourgeois world: but in the violence of their rejection, aren't they also vomiting up the world itself? Ecstasy, orgasm and death, nirvana and despair are all mingled, in this profound and obscure impulse of their entire beings, in their extraordinary vigil beside the sea . . . There is a portent, yes, a portent, of the death or mutation of our world, in their auto-rejection outside of society, in these cells which are at once embryonic and spent, on this last and first shore . . . .

On the freeway going home, the four or five skyscrapers downtown are all lit up, and among them a yellow and mauve, ethereal building, strangely poeticizes the night.

THE CHILDRENS' CRUSADE

They've gone. Where?

On a trip!

Everything revolves around cars and drugs. Marie-Christine and Matthew hitchhiked from New York to San Diego. Carloads of young people meet on the road, exchanging grass. They got a lift from Saint Louis (Missouri) all the way to Los Angeles from some runaway high school boys who, on reaching the coast, wrote a postcard to their families saying that they were never coming home.

What an incredible calling this is! Is it the same one that stirred the teenager from Charleville and the old man of Yasnaya Polyana, and is always stirring me? But this is something stronger, more primitive . . .

Is it disgust, suffering? Candor? "Paradise now"?

How incredible: never before in history have we seen, associated with such naïve, infantile and profound unconscious force, this *severance from the family unit, in an attempt to create a new unit, out of hope or despair: the commune.*

Can I feel, and understand this force? I understand the call for revolution. In fact I understand it even better now than I ever did before: it's the call for mutation. They don't know it, but they know! Revolution! Lenin, Trotsky, Rosa, Mao, could all be said, at certain moments, to have understood the word in all its force, as anthropological mutation. I am far less sensitive to the appeal of drugs. Or rather, what I understand of this appeal (without really feeling it) is counterbalanced by my fear (fear of a bad trip, which is a fear of myself, of my own hidden depths) and by the knowledge that after the experience and the ecstasy, drugs (I mean real drugs, not marijuana or mescaline) lead rapidly to degradation, subjugation, mindlessness.

(For me, Eros is the (only?) path to ecstasy, the real trip).

What I do understand is the inner experience, the break with the flat and conventional world, with the mediocrity of the day-to-day; the quest, in fact, for the true self and the true life. Here, drug culture and the Zen or Krishna approach are part of the same great Messianic wave. It is indeed a search for ecstasy, for paradise now, by chemical means.

Yes, an Elohistic force is at work, here.

In New York, the history professor said an idea was gaining ground among the students: that reason is not the instrument we need in order to live and to survive. Is that the right way to put it?

Ocean Beach: the junkies. Mission Bay: the others.

COMMUNES

Already, the movement is spontaneously developing into an existential-socio-economic network.

The existential communes now being established are becoming work communes: there are farms where the work of cultivation is done using rustic (organic, non-intensive) methods; there are centers for neo-artisanal craft-work (hand-weaving, making things out of leather, etc.), bookshops, and so on. I'm suddenly struck by the thought that this neo-archaic development could be entirely taken over by the commune movement: in fact, this is what will have to happen if the movement is to survive without becoming denatured.

ME

Am too old for the young, too young for the old, and not adult in the least. How do I manage to persist, to survive? Only through my friendships.

What is complementary to me is alternative to others. Some of them are on one side of my valley, the rest are on the other. I am only incompletely understood; so they see me as an incomplete thinker. I do not answer their problems, they do not answer mine. I envelop them in my system, they dislocate mine, and only take up parcels of it, which means they reject what is essential. And yet I can't really complain too much. I could have been crushed, cursed. But the little that I have makes me want more. I want to be considered a sage, a patriarch, a great author. Like the others, I am like the others. I want my name to mean something to people. Look at it, that's your wisdom, you stupid old fool: grotesque and inflated vanity.

DEPRESSION

S. was depressed for three months, shut himself up in his room, saw nobody; then he resurfaced, and went back to his futile life as a manager, the same as before.

DEATH

Death: Interpretations, edited by Hendrick M. Ruiterbeck (an Original Delta edition).

At the New York meeting, the young sociologist Wenglisky proposed, in all seriousness, and with great conviction, that we should found a committee for the abolition of death. This reactivates my desire for a new edition of *L'Homme et la mort.*[16]

INDIANS

Read Stan Steiner's *The New Indians.*
No news of Alanys.

TRANSDUCTION

The word *transduction* (the penetration of a substance from one body into another) pleases, excites, and enchants me.

ME (AGAIN)

Between the anarcho-subjectivist pole and the Hegelian-objectivist pole, I wander ceaselessly; restlessly. Here again, I am as stubborn as the devil in my refusal to elect one of the two philosophies, to enter into alternatives.

EAST–WEST

The daughter of the ex-*Pontifex Maximus* of Polish Marxism is studying here, at the University of San Diego. Kolakowski is at Berkeley, Svetlana Stalin at Princeton.

But the New Left here is drinking up Marxism, clinging to a vulgate that has lost all meaning in the USSR. The news can't have reached them.

SVETLANA

I often think, with veritable fascination: Stalin's daughter is here in America. It's an episode that shows what Shakespearean stuff world history is made of. It's an enlightening episode, whose dim glow, which is all they can perceive of it, is unbearable to the moles. I've already talked about this. I'm reminded, today, of what B. said to me when I asked him if he had read *Letters to a Friend.*

He (looking somber): "I know, you see, from a reliable source, that she is mentally ill . . . So I cannot read that book . . . "

ADVERTISING

On TV, in succession, advertisements for brands of cigarettes and advertisements against cigarettes from the association for the prevention of cancer and heart disease.

EL SOMBRERO

The MacAllisters took us to this Mexican restaurant, in the center of La Jolla. We suddenly find ourselves in an oasis: everybody's talking, going from table to table; the owner plays the guitar. Groups shout across to each other in Spanish. Red wine flows freely. Strangers and friends buy each other rounds. It's pure joy. As the guitar rings out, Johanne leaps up, dances. *Baila*! *Baila*! *Morena*! Next to me a young Mexican yells: *Goza* (enjoy it, enjoy your dance). Then he shouts to me: "*Acabala*" (finish her off)!

DEATH (ADDENDUM)

I should have noted, alongside Wenglisky's proposal, a passage I read in Gordon Rattray Taylor's *The Biological Time-bomb*: "These days, we are seeing the creation of more and more associations for people suffering from sclerosis and other fatal illnesses . . . These organizations . . . see to it that research and treatment are not neglected . . . At the political level, they could play a role as important as that of the trades unions in the past." In the United States, societies for the prolongation of life are also springing up.

SYNCRETISM

Even when the scholastic straitjacket of Marxism or Leninism is already in place, one can identify echoes in revolutionary declarations here that come from elsewhere. For instance, in the article in the *San Diego Free Press* on Brother Fred Ahmed Evans, who faces death in the electric chair for his participation in the street battle of Glenville, Cleveland (23 July 1968): "His actions and his words are an inspiration to those who have not attained *the state of love and revolutionary grace* to which he has risen." In the *Berkeley Tribe* (I think), a White Panther proposes an analysis of American capitalism based on a quotation from William Burroughs, in which capitalism is described as an addiction provoking an excessive secretion of adrenaline, and thus perverting the body's internal economy.

PSYCHEDELIC SHOP

In the psychedelic shop in La Jolla, where we go to collect our tickets for Sunday's concert, there are leather hides, Indian jackets, records, free press publications, and countless varieties of hash-pipes and cigarette papers for marijuana; they also discreetly sell illegal grass. The girl who runs the store, when she's not at the checkout, does craft work on a little workbench behind the counter. She tells us that she's going to hitch-hike around Europe and North Africa with her baby and her husband this summer. She suddenly gets worried when she sees me writing something down in my notebook. But I was just afraid I'd forget an idea, which occurred to me while I was listening to her. She'd been saying to us, with great simplicity, that all human beings are brothers, that humanity should be one big family. I was astonished to hear her speak these truths, which are so evident, so elementary, but have never been felt so profoundly nor so continuously. Here, there are thousands, tens of thousands, even hundreds of thousands of people who feel them profoundly and continuously, and I said to myself that they are reaching the point of mutation, the point of revolution. And suddenly, the opposite idea occurred to me, and that's what I wrote down: "They are reaching the point of revolution. They understand that all Men are the same, that they form a common humanity. But in the absence of any actual event, the mutation fails to take place. And so they will either be reintegrated into society, or absorbed by religious sects, and the most ardent of them will come to believe that Marxism-Leninism provides the practical method of bringing about the transformation." (Profound feeling that here "Marxism-Leninism" is less a theoretical progression than a rationalizing, dogmatic, one-dimensional regression, succeeding an extraordinary moment of existential advance . . .)

Mutation: Does biology hold the key? Are we here, in the Salk Institute, that Sinai-esque blockhouse, in one of the high places where the mutation is being prepared? In any case, Jonas Salk is certainly conscious of and indeed obsessed by the necessary mutation.

I will speak later of my conversation with Salk, in New York.

SCIENTOLOGY

Puerile Scientology (I haven't stuck my nose into it yet)! This philosophy of applied religion expresses – in a naïve and silly form, of course – an aspiration for the doctrine that must one day connect science, philosophy and religion.

BILLY GRAHAM

This evening, the TV broadcasts the latest of the mass sermons, held in the gigantic Anaheim stadium, from Billy Graham's "Crusade" in California. I'm expecting to see some Hollywood-style advertising executive, and I prepare myself for a good laugh. At first, I find him flat; a mere smooth-talker. But then he launches into a kind of incantatory lecture on the theme of bloodshed. Why do all religions emphasize blood? Why does the Bible ceaselessly demand blood? Why did God turn his back on Cain's offering of vegetables and delight in Abel's animal sacrifice? Why did he ask Abraham to sacrifice the blood of his son? Why did Jesus allow his own blood to be shed? *Blood, Blood, Blood,* the word is repeated in a cabalistic chant; his lips pronounce it with something like ecstasy, and he looks like a man possessed. We seem to be on the brink of apocalypse . . . But we stop short. Instead of announcing the great sacrifice, with its torrents of redemptive blood, Billy Graham changes direction, and gives us the Hollywood happy ending: forgiveness, humanity issuing from one blood, that of Adam. The blood which at one point in his sermon was sweeping along the sins of the world (that word, *sin*, how lovely it sounds to my ears!) becomes the wine of the Eucharist.

STRUCTURE AND ELOHIM

What structural theory could ever explain the thirst for blood, the hysteria in Billy Graham's sermon, the frenzy, the ecstasy, the delirium . . . ?

MARCUSE

Dinner at the Marcuses' house yesterday evening. Still the same old adolescent. Almost straight off the bat, he asks me: "So, what can we do? What's the point of working?" and I answer, half-jokingly, that we should now be busy preparing the biological mutation of humanity.

Then we stop talking about important things.

Wednesday, 8 October

Throughout history, all the normal social processes have been disrupted, transformed, and destroyed by wars, invasions and massacres (and this is why we must return to a history of events).

For the first time, Man (science) is capable of total destruction (the H-bomb), and of completely transforming humanity (the biological revolution). "Death and Transfiguration:" the dawn of this third millennium is being played in to the strains of Nietszche and of Richard Strauss.

READING BRONOWSKI

"Man is the solitary social creature."

"The concept of science is neither absolute nor eternal."

Brono shows (in *Science and Human Values*) that every time science makes progress it establishes a link between two heterogeneous domains (Newton: an apple falling and the rotation of the moon around the earth; Faraday: electricity and magnetism; to which Maxwell adds light; Einstein: time and space, mass and energy). Yet to be established is a link between science and magic (this work has already been begun by Lévi-Strauss).

INVENTION

I read, still in Brono, that Newton was 22 years old in 1665; an outbreak of the plague had obliged the University of Cambridge to close. Newton stayed home for eighteen months, far away from official education at a time when he was thirsty for knowledge, *and these are the circumstances in which he saw the apple fall.*

I like the fact that it was the closure of the university that unlocked Newton's genius. Reading Watson's *The Double Helix,*[17] one sees clearly that the official scientific institution is only useful insofar as it can be contradicted and circumvented. Cheating with research subjects, getting by despite the stupidity of anonymous commissions ("a goodly number of scientists are . . . stupid," p. 14), such are in fact the conditions upon which invention depends. Watson reveals the massive role played by interpersonal relationships in this supposedly objective domain. He confirms the superiority of "common sense" reflection in calculation. Of his first intuition of the double helix structure, he writes: "The idea was so simple that it had to be right" (p. 114). Later on, he also says that "a structure this pretty just had to exist" (p. 205).

Yes indeed, it's so simple! And at the same time what complexity! Just look at this Jacob's ladder: it's a spiral staircase! What's this typed copy on deoxyribonucleic paper? Where's the author hiding? Is he dead? Is he taking a nap in a corner? But why look for him at the origin? He's here, among us, within us. The very source of life is stirring, it's at work, structuring and de-structuring, whirling, in our own selves, in our dreams . . .

NEW YORK

As soon as I see Manhattan erect and gray, in a fog itself gray-blue, delight tugs at my heart. It's so beautiful! But would I be able to write about New York, as Stanley suggests . . .

(Speaking of Stanley, I thought he was an Irish Catholic, of proletarian origin; he is of proletarian and Irish origin, but he's Jewish; I tell him I'm disappointed).

Is it because I now love something human in America? New York seems to me less violent, more gentle . . . It's a projection of course. In fact, the danger zones are spreading . . . I pass an old woman in the street who's been mugged and is still bleeding.

But there's the weekend oasis of Central Park. Wonderful hours spent here with Stanley. We see people playing games, football, judo; horses and bicycles circulate in this realm closed to cars for forty-eight hours. Picnics, groups, couples on the grass. Pleasant mild weather, the pleasure of living. Around the bandstand, where a mixed-race group is playing (they're very good), is a gathering of neo-Rousseauian adolescents, in jeans, Indian leathers, hobo gear or party clothes; they give serene and lovely smiles of greeting, as I'd already seen in Los Angeles. Black men and women are curly-haired, solar, some in multicolored African dashikis. Mixed couples. One shade of skin attracts its complementary. The feeling that here, and among themselves, the young have resolved the race problem.

Impression that there are more mixed couples in the Village.

On the first evening, John and I walk down 8th Avenue, still in suits and ties. They look at us in the same way they look at gringo tourists in the working-class districts of Latin America. Now and then, they ask us for "some change" as if it was a tax we owed them. At the junction of 3rd Avenue or Broadway, a Black man shouts at us: "Do you know how much I earn a year, gentlemen? Two dollars!"

THE FISH-TANK

At V. and A.'s place, on 10th street. Their psychedelic pad is a sort of twilight patio, with lush plants, two parrots, two mysteriously illuminated fish-tanks in which bubbles of oxygen rise continually; they pass me a joint of special Kashmiri, then another high-grade opiated hashish. One record plays after another. I'm lying on the bed, which is on the floor, Japanese style; people come in, have a few tokes, leave again. A young girl is there, smiling; four hours go by without me noticing.

I'm fascinated by the big tank: there are exotic fish of all kinds in it, a splendid swishing Chinese angel, two transparent fish whose bones show as if under X-ray, an incredible red-colored fish, others still; all of them are peaceful, and seem to live in idleness, harmony and peaceful coexistence. Only one fish is agitated, he has moustache-antennae like Salvador Dali, but even longer, and he rushes furiously around the tank without taking a moment's rest. When I express my astonishment, A. explains that this fish eats the others' "poo-poo;" he keeps the tank impeccably clean, and the water never needs changing. I wonder vaguely about the use this coprophagous fish makes of his own poo-poo; I marvel at the fact that his Dalinian overexcitement is due only to his healthy appetite. Thus, the tank is a world in equilibrium and quite literally in a sealed jar. I'm delighted to see such happy race relations between these different species; what, not the least little conflict? A. tells me that there have been battles, hatred, jealousy, and even, on the part of the beautiful Chinese angel, attempted infanticide.

But A. brought peace to his little world by spiking the tank with LSD. After a period of undoubtedly ecstatic stupor, the fish became peaceful and carefree. A. also cured one of his parrot's aggressive tendencies with LSD. LSD seems to be his universal panacea. He tells me that he has also been transformed and improved by LSD himself. Before, he was nervous, unstable, anxious. Now, he feels good. He tells me that LSD also did a lot for V. (Indeed, I remember that they became almost mystically united during an unforgettable trip). He assures me that there are no bad trips. – "But . . . " "It's when the ego is bad that bad trips happen". It's not LSD, it's the ego that's to blame. His psychedelic philosophy is based on the opposition of the ego (bad) to the mind and soul. LSD opens the mind. (Gestures with his hands, arms opening windows, which he repeats several times). And I listen, consenting to this philosophy which recognizes several entities in the self, skeptical only about the solution. At about one in the morning, I'm hungry; I manage to get to my feet and stand without losing my balance.

Reunion with the Y. family. Met Alex in the Village. H. is in San Francisco, Ve. in Japan. Vi. is in Geneva at the CERN.

On Tuesday, we're going to see H. in Frisco. Immense pleasure to speak to her on the telephone. I have the feeling we've evolved in the same direction.

RENAULT

Suddenly, on 5th Avenue, I seized a fleeting thought whose presence in me I found astonishing. In fact, I would have been entirely unconscious of this thought if it hadn't caused me a disagreeable sensation, which attracted my attention to my interior monologue. This is what happened. I must have seen a Renault go by and felt very annoyed that there are so few Renaults and so many VWs in the United States. My annoyance turns to the state-controlled management and I curse inwardly: "Those stupid bastards were incapable of taking advantage of the massive American market!" It's at this moment that I overhear myself, and I'm astounded to discover that I have this kind of feeling, that I talk this way, that this is flowing like a river within me, without my even realizing it.

At the One Fifth Avenue Hotel, I had a room on the sixteenth floor, with a balcony looking down on Washington Square and over the skyscrapers of Lower Manhattan, silhouetted against a great big sky.

THE NEW YORK CONFERENCE

Between the 2nd and the 4th of October, the Salk Institute invited twenty people to the Harvard Club, in New York, to discuss *The Entry of Biology into Humanistic Studies*. Some are biologists, but there are also historians, literary specialists, and sociologists. Salk, Bronowski, John, Meyer Shapiro, and George Steiner are there, as well as others who I will more or less get to know. In fact the real problem is: what is Man, what's he going to do, what will the results of the biological revolution be, what can we do about them? Well, this chain of questions, which is the most important of all, doesn't even achieve an approximation of a mutually acceptable answer, but instead reveals the magnitude of all the divisions: the division between scientists and literary specialists, between Europeans and Americans, between theoreticians and practitioners, between the old and the young, between those who have some political experience and those who have none at all, between those who've done their stint with Marx and those who continue to ignore him. The Tower of Babel, someone mutters to me, but one in which we all apparently speak the same language – we just attribute different meanings to the words. (And I think:

in an epoch before mutation, all the key words are emptied of their substance, and become hollow shells; meanings abandon their old carapaces, before their new envelopes have been constructed. It's true that ideas shed their skins, like reptiles or crustaceans).

Once again, I'm amazed by the mutilations that result from alternative thinking. For the young, urgent political questions relegate theoretical problems to the background. For the others, theoretical problems anaesthetize political problems.

As far as the question of the nature of Man is concerned, the zoomorphic approach[18] can't communicate with the anthropocentric approach, nor can the structural approach communicate with the phenomenal approach.

More than ever, I believe we should conceive of humanity as a tripartite entity: species, individual, and society. Man is the subject of biology, psychology, and sociology, which we should not think of as adjacent domains, but rather as manifestations of the same reality. Anthropological identity in its strict sense (with respect to the biological medium) is not some particular distinctive trait; rather, it is a range of more or less distinctive traits, which together account for Man's singularity. Thus, it is not only by his use of tools and his brain that Man is identifiable, as was said in the past, and not only by language, as is said today, but also by magic, myth and the trauma that death inflicts on the most intimate part of his consciousness. And it is this magico-religious Man, the one who finds death unbearable, that is being glossed over today. Man is a neurotic animal, oscillating between the reality of his illusions and the illusion of reality, and is therefore irreducible to a "balanced" model: but both anthropologies and archaeologies have completely forgotten this fact.

(And I really must get cracking on anthropology, for God's sake).

(I'll talk about language later. Two weeks ago I was converted, and now I'm convinced that it's the hub between *bios* and *anthropos*, and that language will allow sociology and biology to be hitched together).

The question of so-called human values brings dissension to its deepest level. Bronowski believes in a re-founding of humanist values, and a reconciliation between art and science; Salk is animated by an extraordinary faith (of which more later): in his view, the biological revolution has been caused by the ground swell of biological evolution itself, because this revolution will realize the necessary mutation of humanity. Steiner takes the opposite view, claiming, in an apocalyptic sermon, that for the first time in history there is a radical contradiction between truth on the one hand, and human hopes and needs on the other. Genetics is destroying our liberal and egalitarian beliefs by demonstrating (??) that there are inequalities, superiorities and inferiorities between the races; there is, according to him, deeper organic satisfaction in masturbation than in copulation (??). Truth is killing us, so to survive must we kill truth? A part of me cries out "yes, yes," while another part of me (as usual) cries out "no, no." Apart from Steiner, and despite the oppositions among them, the others all behave as if science should devote itself to serving "values," as if science distilled values, ignoring the fact that science nihilistically destroys the foundation upon which values are based. Those under thirty want science to be the New Left. And yet they are the only ones, along with Salk, who have any idea of the implications and the political commitment in which biology is already engaged. Wenglisky, the young sociologist, feels that the life and death of humanity are at stake; he becomes inspired, and declares, almost shouting: "We want to survive." (And in the background I hear the voice of the new pre-mutant generation: "*We want to live another kind of life!*") He says, and I think this sentence is fabulous: "We don't want to build nuclear bunkers to protect ethics." (He's the one who'll suggest the creation of a committee for the abolition of death at the end of the meeting).

Thus:

1. There is still no recognized, accepted concept of Man, although, despite and because of the fact that all the sciences, including those of Man, have made astonishing progress.

2. As far as "values," or morality are concerned, there are no theoretical-philosophical bases which everyone finds acceptable, there is no consensus.

In these circumstances, what should be done?

1. I think that we should promote (the Salk taking the initiative?) an anthropo-socio-biological parliament for theoretical reflection on the theme: "What is Man?"

2. Although we cannot found a moral code, discuss values, etc., we can look at some answers to the question: "What should Man be?" and already attempt to conceive of a *model*. What kind of Man do we want? What new relationship should we establish between the individual, the species, and society? This question, which is already the key question of policy at the developmental stage, will become operational when intervention in the brain and genetic intervention begin; it's not only an intellectual and moral question, but also a physical, drive-related, sexual one.

3. At the political level, these scientists are in disarray. Some of them simply want to become advisors to the Prince, warn him of the risks, and guide him onto the right path. The others would like to enlist science as a militant for the New Left. Some still think intervention should only be resorted to in the case of biological weapons (germ warfare and other

kinds) or birth control. I daren't formulate my thoughts, although the need for an anthropolitics seems even more pressing to me here than elsewhere.

And so here I find myself at the heart of all the problems, of all my problems, which have taken on an extraordinary virulence since I've been in California, at the Salk.

CRISIS STUDIES

Some convergence. Wenglisky proposes the creation of "disaster studies" (covering urban pollution, the destruction of natural equilibrium, etc.). I am increasingly convinced that we should create a crisology. I'm confirmed in this opinion by Salk, who tells me that, in biology, *it is in abnormal circumstances that we can discover what a living being is, and it is therefore such circumstances which reveal to us the possibilities inscribed in the phylum.*

CONVERSATION WITH SALK

During the meal at the Harvard Club, I get to know Jonas Salk better. He is as I'd sensed him to be. A philosopher of life, not of vague Teilhardo-Bergsonian vitalism, but of the dialectical "wisdom" incorporated within the original living structure. Everything suggests that "wisdom" in concentrated form is alive even at the organizational level of the most elementary cells, which include both molecules that learn and molecules that preserve. The latter are designed to perpetuate the very structure of the living being, of the particular species, while the mission of the former is to help a being adapt to its environment, or better, to allow it to modify itself.

Learning and unresponsiveness are two contradictory reactions, contradictorily coupled, within the living being, which are always ready to enter into conflict and to act whenever chance, an event, or a threat appears. Both are oriented toward survival, one through useful modification, the other by maintaining the integrity of the structure. Life is the dialectic between these two terms: Conservation and evolution.

Conservatism and evolutionism both project into the future; conservatism is not focused on the past, as Roman Zimand already noted, but is focused on perpetuation, on the indefinite future; evolution, on the other hand, makes a twin response to the future: it both reacts to modifications in the environment, and brings about the progress or development of the being, sometimes separately, and sometimes simultaneously.

Jonas Salk has a very clear sense that there is a dual unity of the *phylum* and the *soma* in Man. The "I" contains the "self" (*phylum*) and the "me"[19] (*soma*), the species and the individual. The "me" lives for the present, the "self" works for the future. This also is the key to life: this dual unity between *the present and the future, this double temporality based on the duality of the genotype-phenotype.*

I say to Jonas: "Maybe it's no accident that the biological revolution is happening precisely when man needs to revolutionize himself."

His face lights up. I've understood him. He is quite convinced that *bios* itself has instigated the biological revolution, that the latter has emerged because man is already in revolution, and that it intends to accomplish this revolution. My anthropolitical intuition, that laboratory procedures do not come from outside to modify the future of the human species, but are on the contrary the internal product of this evolution, is concordant with his fundamental idea. He might almost be saying that the human mind, from the pinnacle of a skyscraper constructed by billions of cells in symphony, and orchestrated by DNA, is stooping to look down at its still active source, in order to discover the secret for new progress. In a sense, DNA is emerging from its secrecy, is beginning its strip-tease under the microscopes of the biologists, because it needs the support of science and technology in order to access a new stage of development.

I cannot say what ecstasy this idea inspires in me. I feel like hugging Jonas . . . Haven't we just been communicating with our aminated matrix? with the MOTHER?

But very quickly his excessive optimism makes me anxious. I tell him that we could also be heading for disaster, for catastrophe. Why of course, he tells me, quite unperturbed, the moment of mutation is always also a time of fragility, of mortal danger, of possible catastrophe. And once again, I'm struck by this mystical feeling I find so enchanting, when the themes of death and rebirth are united.

I am more than ever convinced that the word "survival" is becoming synonymous with the word "revolution," that the word "revolution" is becoming synonymous with the word "mutation." We are approaching a threshold where the questions of survival, mutation, and revolution will become the same and the only question.

For my part, I feel anxious and hopeful at the same time, I sense obliteration on the prowl at the same time as new life. But Jonas is the prophet of Life. God is in the genes. Genes bear God within them. On a scrap of paper, I write him: ADN,[20] DNA : ADoNai, aDoNAi. And it's true: God, principle of Creation and principle of the beyond, really is the Life principle that we carry within us . . .

Monday 13 October

DEL MAR

Home to freaks; something disheveled about it, which gives an impression of being in the countryside, of peace . . .

LOS ANGELES

Eight million cars.

From time to time, when the degree of pollution in the atmosphere rises above a certain level, a siren sounds the smog alert.

POLLUTION

It's a real theme (the pollution of rivers, lakes, oceans, the pollution of harvests by pesticide, air pollution in urban areas), which is becoming obsessive, symbolic, metaphysical, prophetic. What it conveys is not so much the failures and disruptions of development as the filth and degradation brought about by the pre-eminence of money and technology.

(It's easy to see how neo-Puritanism and neo-Rousseauism have been able to converge on the theme of pollution).

DDT the savior has become DDT the poison. DDT destroys the ability to photosynthesize, hence all plant life, and hence Life itself.

In the September issue of *Ramparts*, Paul Erlich's article, entitled "Eco-Catastrophe"; it's half science fiction, predicting the death of the ocean in 1979 as a result of worldwide pollution.

These warning cries, instead of worrying me, reassure me, because they mean that a problem is being recognized, and therefore that the preliminaries for corrective action are in place. What worry me are the problems that haven't been announced with cries of warning. What worries me is not the ecological threat, it's the threat from within.

But perhaps the threat of external pollution expresses, by projection, the internal pollution with which this civilization feels itself to be contaminated?

RON

After receiving his Ph.D. in Economics, Ron gave up his career to become a schoolteacher in a Black neighborhood in Oakland.

This boy's profound satisfaction at having rejected a technocratic profession, and devoted himself to the children of the ghetto. He has sensed his truth, and I feel it too, so evident, with no need of ideological rationalization.

EVOLUTION–REVOLUTION

All the trends that are asserting themselves in the cultural revolution already existed in society, as counter-trends (neo-naturism, neo-Rousseauism, neo-archaism), in which we used to immerse ourselves on an alternate basis (during our leisure time or holidays). The cultural revolution replaces the alternate with the alternative.

Neo-tribal culture: neo-Rousseauism + neo-archaism + McLuhanism.

ANTI-BOURGEOIS AND META-BOURGEOIS SOCIETY

It became clear to me, while talking to Alain Touraine in Los Angeles, that the development of the new (tribal, hippie, communal) culture has found its natural economic basis in the neo-cultural, neo-artisanal and neo-archaic sectors (troubadours, musicians, photographers, hawkers, artisans, jewelers, weavers, coffee-sellers, farmers, etc.), which are being developed, as a necessary counter-weight, by the contemporary course of industrial-urban civilization itself.

Thus, the social basis for the revolution may not be made up of Serge Mallet's beloved neo-technicians, the engineers-cum-office workers, who are not yet capable of living and experimenting with new mores: in fact, it may come from the "freaks", who derive their economic support from sectors outside the circuit of rationalization and industrial mass production.

In this way, the counter-society could cease to be parasitic, and may therefore avoid auto-disintegration. Its economy would be at once antagonistic and complementary to the bourgeois economy, just as the latter was for a few centuries in relation to the feudal economy.

In parallel, the new culture, which has already partially emerged in the marginal sections of society,[21] is now ready to undertake a thorough colonization of the intelligentsia: that is, of a growing class whose role in society is becoming increasingly important. It could infiltrate the University, and the research centers and institutions. It could establish itself within the scientific avant-garde. (Already in the U.S. there are laboratories where researchers are absolutely free to use their time as they desire and to work on whatever they want).

At the same time, new Foundations could also develop (Crisis Centers, Whole Earth Catalogue, etc.) and form federations with each other.

Reflect on all of this: multiple infiltrations are possible; innumerable pseudopodia could join up and close together above and beneath the bourgeois-bureaucratic-technocratic world.

This may be Utopian, but it's not nearly as insane as putting our hopes in the old or new working class.

THE FIRST WAVE

The first spring is fading, the first wave is dying . . . From the outside, the "pigs" are exercising increasingly brutal repression, they're tightening their control, and this is accentuating, even determining, the process of auto-degradation. Drug abuse on one side, and Marxism-Leninism (the alternative drug) on the other, are destroying the great crusade of love from within: both, in their different ways, are derailing this extraordinary rebellion.

ROCK FESTIVAL AT THE STADIUM

On Sunday, between 11 a.m. and 7 p.m., several thousand adolescents gather on the lawn of the stadium, along with 10 to 12-year-old kids, young parents with their children, and dogs. As we go in, we're stopped and searched by the police: they confiscate three cans of beer (alcohol is prohibited). On the highest tiers of the stadium, here and there, stand the "pigs;" there are not many of them, but they're making their presence felt. It's like being on a temporary reservation, within the hollow of this stadium; we're free inside it, but our freedom is under surveillance.

There's a huge picnic going on the grass. Plumes of marijuana smoke rise. From noon onwards, guys and (very young) girls begin to get sick; they're led off to the little makeshift clinic run by the Crisis Center, which announces its presence over the P.A., addressing itself in code to those who are "suffering from the heat." There are stalls, some selling hippie craftwork, with jewelry, leather, clothes, cigarette papers for marijuana and pipes for hashish; others are political. The Maoists are displaying a color portrait of Chairman Mao. The SDS (Students for a Democratic Society) is selling Marxist literature. The Black Panther Party stall is offering Black revolutionary writings, the classic pamphlets by Lenin and Marx, and Mao's little book. Religious stalls propose various biblical panaceas. People, apparently commune members, are gathered around other stalls and pass joints to one another. Totems are planted here and there on the lawn, each with a few people standing next to it. The Vietnamese flag is flying somewhere up on the tiers. Two big flags over the orchestra pit, one psychedelic, a jumble of bright colors, with the peace sign in the middle, the other plain white, bearing the same symbol.

Some girls are wearing dresses made out of American flags. There are a few really fanciful outfits, but the hobo uniform predominates: faded, patched, even torn blue jeans. The symbol of austere refusal and extreme poverty has taken precedence over free, bright, cheerful costume. The happy spring of 1966 to 1968 is far away . . . In fact, there's a sadness here, which Johanne senses very strongly. The drugs no longer induce euphoria; these people are crushed, prostrate. I realize that *they are lost*. Is it because the ebb of the cultural revolution is laying bare the terrible sorrow of these young people, who are both the poorest and the richest in the world?

Or rather, on the one hand there is hope, the search for a different kind of life, the desire to live in love, and then at the same time there is despair . . .

What is apparent in this stadium, while the first groups play, not yet arousing collective fervor, is above all a sense of *togetherness*. All these misfit cells from the great social body, these escapees from the great organism, are assembling, coagulating, they want to form a new body, they're waiting for illumination, for the flash of light.

They look serious, almost numb. When you smile at them, their faces light up with those marvelous smiles that tore through my anti-American membrane.

Time passes, and Johanne feels anxious that she can't do anything for these boys and girls who drug themselves in misery. A group onstage has lost its musicians, some of whom are stoned out of their minds. A guy walks across the lawn ringing a little bell, calling, like a wandering peddler: "LSD, acid." Is it a joke? Johanne wants to leave. I move closer to the group for a moment, where the manic dancers have gathered, packed together, in the deafening din of sixteen six-stacks of amplifiers, arranged in a continuous line of fire. Intoxication seizes me, and I go and writhe with them for a while. From time to time, a magical whooping rises up around the band, like the cries of spirits in the sacred forest. Incredible archaism. That's what I love.

NIGHT BEACH

The night before, at about half past midnight, we were on our way back from the Forresters', mildly high, and we decided to go for a walk on the beach. We saw shadows running, appearing, disappearing; then we were drawn to the glow of a bonfire: two teenage couples were roasting marshmallows. They make an offering of marshmallows, I give them cigarettes, we talk about France, and America.

They're students. We point out our house to them and invite them to come and see us.

What Elohim is calling these youngsters in their thousands to the beaches, to this shore beside the sea, to wait there as if in preparation for a fantastic journey, as if they'd come in search of the symbol of freedom and of the original confusion of all things, the open sea? What is it? What is it?

There are hundreds of them, on Ocean Beach and Pacific Beach. They're camping out, waiting.

WOODSTOCK

Saw the special issue of *Life* on Woodstock. There were between 300 and 500 thousand of them, they joined forces, they came together, they listened to music, there was no violence; two people died, two children were born.

THE SMILE

I've found the exact expression for my rapture and my anguish at the Los Angeles park-in: the smile she gave me was so engaging that it was hard for me not to respond to it.

SECURITY

Their parents no longer make them feel secure, instead they make them anxious, and so they run away from them. Why isn't parental love reassuring any more? Why do children go looking for security in collective love? The clan, the tribe, are being reborn as the family crumbles. But why have family structures broken down so completely and so suddenly?

Love is my only security.

HELL'S ANGELS

There were a few of them at the stadium, potent and terrifying to behold, wearing their worn-in leathers, with the insignia on their backs, some of them displaying very beautiful colored tattoos.

Mathilde met a guy from the Mezcalera gang in a nightclub on the coast. He was between 25 and 28 years old, wearing a swastika, a tattoo, and a badge inscribed with the figure 13/69. He explained: every time he's eaten pussy, which in America as in France is called 69, he's had bad luck, and been arrested shortly afterwards. Hence the number 13, symbol of misfortune. His friends nicknamed him 13/69.

He told her that he'd never have talked to a girl like her five years ago, he'd have robbed and/or raped her. But, he explained, he and his friends are gentler now. They don't need to rob and pillage any more; film directors come and pay to make movies about them, and journalists pay them for interviews; they each have two or three women working for them . . . Besides, drugs have made them soft. They don't want to fight any more, they don't hate society any more, they've even lost their sexual prowess: "All I've got between my legs these days is marshmallow."

But apparently there are still gangs that hold up grocery stores inland. The police let them get away with it, says Mathilde. (*Modus vivendi*?)

HIGH

Since I've been here, I've been intellectually high.

HELENE

The seeds of a very close friendship, formed thirty years (thirty years!) ago in Toulouse, and since then buried in the unvisited layers of memory; but here they are again, reawakened in both of us as soon as we spoke on the telephone.

ME

I am increasingly astonished, and by everything. I am astonished that other people aren't astonished, but also my own astonishment astonishes me.

SUN

This evening, another magnificent sunset.

COSMOS

This strange guy, at the Forrester's, suddenly told us that humanity's absolute priority is to establish colonies on Mars. Famine in India, under-development, all those things are secondary. We must avoid the atomic destruction of the human species, which is an increasing danger as long as humans live on this planet alone. Mars is of interest, not in itself, but because it is a stage on the way to Alpha Centauri.

"Mars is uninhabitable," someone says.

He retorts triumphantly:

"The first explorers of California said that it was an uninhabitable desert."

I try to assemble my arguments to suggest that the civilization of the planet and the conquest of space should be viewed as complementary, and not as alternatives; then I give up.

The real challenge is that of cosmic death. All Man can do is create the *metanthropos*, who in turn will create someone or something to fight against cosmic death.

CREATION AND EPILEPSY

Mutation, creation, procreation (making love) are, each in its way, moments of epilepsy.

(Mutation: the most profound mystery lies in this creative epilepsy of the structure: it is in the epileptic structure that the secret is to be found).

Epilepsy: a return to the original chaos from which the new structure is born.

(Article in the *New York Review of Books*, "Much Madness." The premise is that the de-structuring processes that can lead to convulsions (epilepsy) are the same ones that can lead to creation).

REVOLUTION

Progression and regression (barbarism) present themselves simultaneously at revolution's door.

POLITICS AND METAPOLITICS

A metaphysical problem and an anthropological problem are emerging in this century alongside the political and social problems. All of these things communicate: the political problem can no longer be dissociated from the philosophical problem or the anthropological problem. I have thought so for a long time. But that doesn't mean we can pass off the metaphysical evil as a political evil, nor the anthropological problem as a social problem . . .

USA

From the beginning, this has been a society, a civilization, with two faces, one of which comes from its foundation in emancipation and decolonization, and its establishment of civil rights, while the other comes from its institutionalization of slavery and its destruction, decimation, of the Indian tribes. This Atheno-Roman duality, which is so unbearable to those who think in alternatives, can still be recognized today in this vast society, in other guises. On the one hand, it's the best society that has ever existed on a massive scale, on the other, it's the worst.

What is happening in the United States is not only fantastic technological and scientific avant-gardism, it's also an extraordinary crisis of civilization, it's the cultural revolution of the young, it's the birth of the African-American nation, of the Indian nation.

It is in California that these metamorphic beginnings are taking place.

BILLY GRAHAM

On Thursday night, I watched another sermon on TV from the Billy Graham crusade. What convinces me that he is more than a mediocre preacher is when he says that America's greatest evil is not corruption or immorality, but *wealth*. He declares that dogs and cats in America live better than most of the humans on the planet. He makes the richest audience in the world smell the stench of money.

(They're going to snigger at me for not sniggering at Billy Graham).

(I'm obsessed with "them," I have to keep fighting against their intimidation).

He brings Pascal's wager up to date, in a way that makes me laugh. He says: "Let's say that there's only a 10 percent chance that hell exists. Would you take a plane at the airport if they told you it had a 10 percent chance of crashing? Well then, take the Lord's plane, and cover the risk . . . "

DON'T CRY, SCREAM

(Title of a collection of poems by a black writer).

SUNSET

(Over to me, Chateaubriand! . . .)

The reddish-orange globe of the sun is plunging rapidly into the water; for an instant, the sunken part seems to continue to shine beneath the ocean: of course, this illusion is created by the reflection on the water of the half-disc which is still visible. A fabulous impression that the sun has gone down to reign over a submarine empire as vast as the sky itself. It's entering the kingdom of Osiris! The cosmos is suddenly transfigured by a violent chromatic revolution. The sea turns an unbelievable mauve. The horizon is a crush of intense colors. All the clouds scattered in the firmament turn pink. But the most beautiful color of all is a pellucid blue, very pale, utterly ethereal, which is consuming the western part of the sky. I look up at this sky, and I see a great gray-blue four-engined jet slip gently by, in silence . . .

(Why do we feel so concerned, so moved, by such spectacles?)

DINNER AT THE KOHNS'

It's a house on a hill, almost completely hidden by trees, near the Rancho Santa Fe. There are orange trees, mangoes, guavas, ducks, turkeys, pheasants, peacocks . . .

I jot down Melvyn's remark on addiction: when morphine injections are given in order to ease extreme physical pain, addiction results in only 1% of cases; however, if the injection is given to procure pleasure, addiction is almost instantaneous.

So it seems that intoxication is a psychological phenomenon.

A far-ranging conversation about time, chance, and evolution. At one point, Suzanne says something that I don't entirely understand, but which I find extremely striking and thought-provoking; what she says, more or less, is that time does not exist at molecular level: what exists is the affinity between two molecules, and time is merely a measurement of this affinity between two molecules, which unite more or less rapidly. She even says, metaphorically, but it's very beautiful coming from her (beautiful) mouth, "affinity, in other words, the love between two molecules."

I sense a division between Melvyn and Maxime on one side, and me on the other, because they think that chance can explain evolutionary phenomena, on the basis of mutations and natural selections. But, I say, what about creativity, what about the *verve* of life ("Nature in her fruitful verve . . . "); their point of view explains the disappearance of species, but not the origin of the wing, the eye, the heart, etc.

Suzanne: "*Life is a balancing act.*"

Suzanne is an exquisite person. He is too, but I am especially sensitive to her, because she is a woman.

(Euchariotic organism. Look into this).

CHEMISTRY

Syntex: an aphrodisiac.

B.H.T.: doubles life expectancy (in mice).

ANTHROPOLOGY

A science of Man that is impervious to dancing, to play, to tenderness, to laughter, is a load of bull.

I'm right to keep putting off anthropology, because I keep learning new things.

THE MODERN ERA

This is the era in which individualism and Communism appear to be the two great contradictory and interdependent necessities.

AMERICAN FASCISM

Up to now, America has not managed to generate its own form of Fascism; it is generating racism, conservatism, anti-communism, and chauvinism, but has not yet been able to mine socialist ideology and the praxis of a disciplinarian-community party, and come up with the fermenting and the cementing agents needed to create "Fascism."

ON THE LEFT

The Angela Davis affair. Fight for her, yes; but not under her banner. Yes to all her criticisms of the American University and politics, but the fact that she's defending freedom by brandishing the Communist flag gives me a very familiar and disagreeable feeling of stupidity and hypocrisy.

Every form of Leftism needs to remember this vital principle: have a little lucidity about so-called socialist regimes, and a basic sense of proportion when comparing oppressions and repressions.

It's as if they want a Fascism of their own.

RATIONALIZATION

Integrating fragmentary information into a coherent whole is a normal thought process; the remarkable thing is that we do it in obedience to a secret desire, and everywhere rationalization claims to be, and believes itself to be, rationality.

SOCIOLOGICAL HOMEOPATHY

A curious article in *Esquire*; it's a report by an academic who wants to remain anonymous, entitled *Toward a Homeopathic Social Science.* Just as homeopathic medicine cures disease by administering small controlled doses of the substance that caused the problem, so we must envisage a homeopathic social science. Thus, in respect of racism: "We now know that racism was an evil when it was not generalized. By inoculating each branch of society with the appropriate type of racism, we will give renewed vigor to the whole of American life." We must oppose the great unilateral racism with little reciprocal forms of racism, which will balance each other out; in the same way, we need to counteract the big ghettoes with small ones, etc.

These are truly desperate remedies, of which we can only despair.

Suddenly, I come across a thought-provoking sentence: "What if our society's problem were not that there is too much violence, but too little?"

SOCIOLOGY

American sociology, which the officials of French sociology still take to be the Tablets of the Law, has disintegrated, Touraine tells me.

He is rather disdainful about the *Economic and Philosophical Manuscripts*, in comparison to the *Manifesto*. I believe, on the contrary, that the manuscript represents the theory in a state of fusion and fission, in its nascent stage.

Study group phenomena (and group structures) in the communes, and examine the variations caused by drugs.

Saturday 18 October

SAN FRANCISCO (14–17 October)

I haven't got a car any more.

I'm driving faster and faster down the freeway, exceeding the 65 mile an hour speed limit; I hit 70, then 75, then 80. Leaving the Sacramento expressway to get on to Highway 5, I fly onto the deserted road. A helicopter spots me, and a police car suddenly appears in pursuit, with its siren screaming, and its red light flashing in my rearview mirror. The irate traffic cop gives me a ticket, and then calms down as I express (feigned) dismay, me being a foreigner, and we say goodbye cordially. Further on, the road narrows into two lanes, and the cars line up behind some enormous tractor-trailers. Just as I'm overtaking one of these monsters, my accelerator jams on the floor and the engine revs wildly. Other cars have pulled out behind me, they're following me, and more trucks are approaching from the other direction. In the extraordinary slow-motion velocity characteristic of accidents, I try ducking down to yank up the accelerator with my right hand, holding the steering with the left, but while my head disappears below the windscreen for a moment and I can't see, the truck in front is advancing relentlessly toward me, and at the same time the rear-view mirror shows other cars that have followed me and are right up behind, and I shout to Johanne to pull up the pedal block, while I try to get this crazy tank under control; Johanne dives down, grabs something, can't do it, meanwhile I've pulled over in front of the truck I was overtaking, and we're hurtling along at breakneck speed, the brakes having failed completely. When I've made a bit of distance, I put the car into neutral, the engine races and squeals, I swerve onto the soft shoulder, braking and switching off the engine as the file of cars rumbles past me. When I set off again, the engine refuses to respond normally and sticks in low gear. So now I've got to drive at less than 40 miles an hour, and the car is overheating. We get to Larkspur in the night and in trouble, having received another ticket, this one for driving too slowly. The next day, I ask several mechanics for a diagnosis, and they all assure me that repairing the transmission would cost me at least the price of the car. Some of them tell me my Chevrolet is shot anyway, that it consumes too much oil, that the engine block would have to be completely changed, etc. In the end, after a final consultation with Nick and with Charlotte's mechanic friend, I mournfully decide to part with my car. It's easy for me to abandon the car as object, but letting go of the car as toy is hard. I have (I still have) brief moments of childish sorrow, thinking of this huge, fabulous moving thing, so wide, so long, with so many features and gadgets, and which I have described in my letters to all my friends in France. Now the young Larkspur hippies can take their turn to play with it. They're going to paint it and make a mobile home out of it.

SEEING H. AGAIN

Four years ago, H. smoked grass for the first time. And she discovered, in a record she had listened to a thousand times, sounds and musical nuances that she had never perceived before; she said to herself that there must be, not only sounds, but colors, perceptions, and feelings, to which she could and should open her mind. She looked at the people around her and saw them differently; she saw pettiness in some and goodness in others, she was horrified by hypocrisy and wanted to live in truth. She was married to a biologist, an extremely nice man, with whom she has remained on excellent terms, and she had four children. She changed her life. She had no desire to escape from her family; on the contrary, she's gotten closer to her children, sharing their philosophy and their spontaneous attitude to life; she has taken her distance from the bourgeois lifestyle, she has ceased to be an academic's wife. Her house in the woods in Larkspur, among the giant trees, has become a hostel open night and day: its door is never closed. H. has taken up weaving, she has installed a loom in one room and has let her inspiration run free; she's been teaching for a year or two in an arts center in M., a hundred miles to the north, on the coast. There was a big commune of young people living there. The house in Larkspur is now a semi-commune. Hippies come, they smoke, paint, draw, make neo-archaic objects, Indian-style. They can shower, sleep, get something to eat. They play drums (there are four African tam-tams in the living room); they play the flute. There's something idyllic, bucolic, extraordinary about this house, which is permeated by freedom and a sense of community. The youngest of H.'s children has built a house hidden in the woods with a friend, where they sometimes go and spend the night; on the night of our arrival, they'd brought back a deer, and the next day they prepared and smoked the animal in the Indian way, with a supplementary seasoning of Mary Jane. All of them seem to live without money, outside industrial civilization, organization, and constraint. Their life is frugal. But some money does come in, either from H.'s weaving, or from what D. pays her in child support; in fact, a few months ago, H. had to establish a basic discipline, which allows her to protect her work, and prevent the house from becoming a slum; I find this symbiosis between two contradictions, spontaneity and order, "one day at a time" and continuity, quite admirable. It's a matriarchal, maternal commune, in which H. is the center of love as well as regulation . . .

The Larkspur house floats on like a little boat, not allowing itself to be capsized by the cultural revolution (I'll have to speak later of the terrible self-destructive force that exists within this creativity). Through her experience, H. has understood that the cultural revolution needs an economic basis, and that it should be neo-artisanal, neo-archaic. She is doing her best to make her work and art, her art and life, coincide . . . .

A coming-together, a synthesis, has been effected between H.'s Russian-ness and Californian hippieism. H.'s mother came to Toulouse as a refugee in 1940; her father, a well-known scientist, died during the exodus; the family was entirely destitute, and lived on the solidarity of university friends. They had no money, and this was the period of rationing, but they kept open house in the rue du Japon. Madame Y. always offered tea, something to eat, and at mealtimes she would always lay a place for visitors. The hospitality of this house was, for me and the friends who went there, fabulous. Madame Y. worked tirelessly, cooking, washing up, doing the laundry, ironing, sewing the family's clothes, joining in the conversations, and she never went to bed before about four in the morning. Violette lived at their place (after H. had left for Marseilles, I think). And now the same house has been reconstituted in Larkspur, but this is a hippie, yankee-fied version, centered on the philosophy that grass opens up the soul and confers the gift of extra-lucidity.

We met Charlotte, Nick, Skyfish and his girlfriend, who are trying their hands at making rings out of leather (Skyfish has also made himself a pair of Indian-style hide trousers). Survivors of the shipwrecked M. commune drop by, taking shelter here when they need it, and others come just to play the drums and the flute.

Three very important days. I am right in the midst of what fascinates me. The first evening, after the trials and tribulations of the journey, is suffused with sweet warmth, being with H. again, the way she is now, now that she has become herself (to evolve is to find oneself), and with young strangers, male and female; she and Johanne strike up an immediate, intense friendship. Yes, we have found our place here.

Peace, joy, we drink wine, we smoke grass, we are together.

H. tells us that the real break, the great transformation came about four years ago, when the experience of smoking grass became widespread. It was a vital experience, which, she believes, changes one's vision of the world. *Farniente*, which the Puritan work ethic equates with idleness and vacuity, has become intensity, plenitude, expansion of the self, brotherhood with others, and communication with the world. This acted as the catalyst, speeding up and spurring on the genesis of neo-Rousseauism and of the new culture, which are interlinked, and are both forms of anthropological feedback provoked by technical-industrial-urban-bourgeois civilization.

Something extremely archaic, a form of neo-tribalism, has sprung up at the most advanced point of modernity. Only a small portion of this neo-tribalism could be called McLuhanian, but this portion does exist (through the influence of the media).

They want to be noble savages, they want to be Indians, they want to be Crusoes and Fridays, they want to be and not to be . . .

Fleeting images: on Friday morning, in front of the house, Nick and Skyfish play the flute, a girl is sewing.

Many of these young people, with their beards and their long hair, have Christ-like faces. They are gentle and serious. Increasingly, I see great sorrow in their seriousness.

A strange aquatic-mobile town in Sausalito. Moored on the water, great floating balloons serve as capsule-habitats. Bizarre encampments form a surrealist shanty town; extravagant flights of fancy have dictated the choice and the combination of construction materials. These are shells for hermit crabs, deliberately fashioned out of the most multifarious constituents. A sort of Disney castle has been erected on an old truck; it has two stories, and is completed by a little medieval tower made of odds and ends. There are old broken-down cars, from which neo-tramps emerge, barefoot . . .

Some of them live on the beaches, some in the woods, others in these shacks . . . All of them are seeking to live frugally, in poverty. They want to get by without dollars, they would almost like to consume nothing at all, yet many of these barefoot urchins still possess what seems a luxury to us, and which, in these sprawling cities, so ill-served by public transport, is more indispensable than a pair of shoes: a car.

Desperate attempts to live without money; some communes practice barter, others live on reciprocal donations, alternating gifts.

The rain, floods of it, began on Tuesday night and lasted forty-eight hours. It flushed out the people living in the woods and on the beaches.

The measure of riches was too great for these children of Puritans, while the measure of poverty in the world, which was revealed to them by the media, was too great for these children of the rich.

They want to live the true life and also to punish themselves for a horrifying sin.

Many are children from rich families. Are they playacting? Yes, in a sense . . . They are playing at poverty, as seriously as possible.

They're jumping out of the plane, equipped with parachutes, of course, but they don't open them. Some of them are crushed when they hit the ground.

They do all they can not to open their parachutes. But they still have them.

Evidently, the privilege of these children of rich parents is that they can be glad to be poor.

Leslek tells me a legend of his own invention: the dolphins once developed a prodigious civilization beneath the ocean, then one day they realized that it was all a complete waste of time. So they abandoned everything and went off to play in the seas; they are, in short, hippies who succeeded.

Analyze the sickness of the super-ego: why has authority lost its authority? As a consequence of "liberalism" (liberalism should be analyzed as a form of semi-authoritarianism). But why, how, did liberalization (of the family, of education) ever come about? Link all this to the crisis of values, examine what the *refusal of the paternal role* means.

WHERE IS THE RUPTURE?

It has been called a counter-culture (Theodore Roszak), but the prefix puts too much emphasis on negation. This is also a cultural revolution, which integrates its own positive values. Some of these values already existed in society, but they were either sealed off as the preserve of children, or experienced as relaxation from the "serious" life of work (in the form of vacations, leisure, play, aesthetics); or else they were contained within the straitjacket of religion, which cut off any possibility of bringing them into communication with everyday life.

1. In one sense, the cultural revolution wants to prolong the child's world beyond childhood; this is the world of Fenimore Cooper's novels, of Uncle Tom's cause, where the Indian and the Black are authentic characters who live in contact with nature; it's also the Disney world where people can speak to the animals and understand them . . . The cultural revolution, like all great revolutions, is the desire to preserve and to achieve an infantile universe of communion and immediacy; hippieism, in one of its profound aspects, is an attempt to realize the child's imaginary world in adolescence, in life.

(Which indicates the path for sociology: find out where, and how, during adolescence, the mechanism that commands the disintegration of childhood values and integration into the values of adult society fails to be activated).

2. Neo-Rousseauism, which already had a strong cultural tradition in the United States, is a counter-current caused by the increasing restrictiveness of modern life. This neo-Rousseauism carries within it the quest for the free and fulfilling life of the body, the repose of the soul, communion with nature, and ARKHE in all of its forms. But it is experienced *on an alternate basis* in adult society. The cultural revolution is the transformation of the alternate into the alternative: false, artificial, rarefied life is opposed to a life in harmony with the nature of Man and with natural Man (cf. the *ecology movement*).

3. As for Christianity, it's the Sermon on the Mount that is making a sudden bid for freedom from the straitjacket of the institutionalized churches. The need for purity and communion, the announcement of the beatitudes for the humble in spirit and in possessions, and the quest for salvation have been revived, are being experienced here and now: *Paradise now!* This profound reincarnation of evangelical values has led to shame and disgust at a life based on egocentricity and self-interest; in other words, at the bourgeois life of White America. In the past, the gospel merely acted as a halo of spirituality for bourgeois materialism; now it has become its operational critique.

4. It could also be argued, partially and in a certain sense, that the individualist, libertarian shoot of the cultural revolution is already present in embryo in the bourgeois individualism of mainstream society. Hedonism, promoted and spurred on by increasing consumption, also extends into the new culture, but it has metamorphosed in the process. The fact is that there is a decisive rupture at the very heart of individualism: the individualism of sensation, pleasure, and exaltation is now opposed to the individualism of property, of acquisition, of possession; consummation is opposed to consumption, and although both are branches that emerge

from the same source, the hedonism of being (cultural revolution) is radically opposed to the hedonism of having (bourgeois society).

The cultural rupture is therefore the sudden manifestation of something that was already present, and sustained, but repressed, curtailed and deflected, within the culture of society itself. And this manifestation has been achieved in and by means of the negation of the repressive and curtailing agent.

5. However, the rupture is also the irruption of revolutionary elements that had previously been rejected outside the social and cultural *lines*. It is the irruption of *communism*, in its double, total, contradictory, confused (but, in anthropological terms, immensely rich and potent) original nature: as both community-oriented and libertarian. This irruption is predominantly existential. Communism is attempting to establish itself as a way of life rather than a theoretical tool. Primarily, it is tending to be embodied within the cultural revolution, and not in the process of a political revolution aimed at seizing State power. Nevertheless, this is indeed communism, in the form in which it appeared, as aspiration and necessity, in the works of Fourier, Proudhon, and Marx.

(At this point, we should try to figure out how cultural elements, which have suddenly become eruptive, and revolutionary themes, which have suddenly become irruptive, intermingle from here on: how the quest for happiness is becoming the aspiration toward another kind of life, the aspiration toward another kind of life is becoming the quest for happiness, the individualist need is becoming anarchist, the need for community is becoming Communist, and all of them are becoming revolutionary).

6. To all these elements of both continuity and rupture, we should add a factor that represents a new ingredient, which was originally foreign to the western world, but is now being translated in their different ways by the Hindu and Buddhist themes, by the fascination with India and Katmandu, and, most powerfully, by the experience of drugs: the quest for the true world concealed beneath the world that only appears to be real, the quest for the inner secrets of the psyche, the quest for communion with Being through the ecstatic life, and even for Nirvanian obliteration. Whereas Communism is a counter-current whose source is in fact the development of the western bourgeois world, what we are seeing here is the ecstaticism of a counter-current which originated elsewhere, but has been snatched up and cried out for from within, as a consequence of the deficiencies of the West, *and is in fact in opposition to westerness*, insofar as westerness means activism, historical dynamism, technicity, rationality and rationalism. Thus, while eastern philosophy is being reabsorbed, is dispersing and drying up in Asia because it hampers the pursuit of the technical adventure, its spores are spontaneously germinating in the Far West,

where the resistance to the disruption and the excesses that have resulted from the technical adventure is emerging . . .

The notion of *Paradise now* represents the point of convergence for primitive neo-Christianity, primitive neo-Communism, and the ecstatic narco-Asiatic quest . . .

Roszak is right to define the "counterculture" as a cultural totality with its own lifestyle, its own sacraments (drugs, sex, rock festivals), its own media (free press, radio stations, films), and its own literature; but we need to extend this definition: it also has its own ontological foundations, and its own embryonic social structure (solidarity networks and communal cells). It has a class basis, constituted by the young and a section of the intelligentsia; it is beginning to have its own economic basis in the neo-craft and neo-archaic sector, which is in fact developing as feedback to the evolution of modern civilization.

Of course, it may all die down, or rather become denatured under pressure from the combined forces of internal decomposition and external repression. But it still represents the inevitable pre-mutation of modern civilization – although civilization may also go backwards, in a vast historical regression, or it may become subject to a new determining factor.

To return to the rupture: it is acute, extensive, and profound here because the US is the most advanced – the most mature – country in techno-urban-bourgeois evolution, and therefore the most likely to experience the first symptoms of the inevitable crisis of civilization earlier and at a deeper level. But there are also other determining factors:

1. The under-civilized or under-policed[22] nature of American society. In the great geo-sociological spaces that have constituted America since its origin, the net cast by the *polis* and the police is much wider and looser than in the old, dense societies of the West. Furthermore, since this is a society marked by Puritanism, its system of repression is initially internal, operating within the conscience of each person, and external repression only begins to act when internal repression has failed. The dwindling of the Puritan conscience, which has been speeding up since the Second World War, has therefore accentuated the laxity characteristic of American society.

This freedom from domination by the *polis* allows us to understand America's two-fold tolerance: a tolerance which on the one hand embraces a measure of violence and criminality, and the jungle chaos which would bring down the entire social edifice elsewhere; and on the other hand a tolerance of anomie, difference, and innovation – as long as they develop on the margins of the *polis*, or are encompassed within the net. Finally, we should add that it has been possible to defend and guarantee freedom, within the zones of tolerance, thanks to the most liberal constitution *for the individual* in the world.

Thus one can see how a new type of counter-social fabric has been able to develop, as if outside territorial limits, and with what almost amounts to internal sovereignty, in Greenwich Village, Haight Ashbury, Sausalito, Taos, and in the communes . . . American society tolerated the formation of hippie communities, and an extraordinary cultural revolution, for a period of three years. A year ago the movement began to be threatened, repressed, and above all contained and surrounded. And the repression has come precisely when the movement, continuing its expansion, and ceasing to be purely and simply a voluntary neo-ghetto, is beginning to gnaw away at all the fibers of society from the inside, at the juvenile level; precisely when the movement is showing itself to be more than an anomic form of deviancy: it is the bearer of norms that are absolutely contrary to the norms of US society; precisely when the un-American nature of the movement is, because of the war it has declared on the "American way of life," becoming anti-American.

2. We should add to this a factor bearing on the relationships between parents and children, and between students and the educational establishment. For twenty or thirty years now, under the conjoined influence of the psychoanalytic vulgate and the hedonistic and neo-Rousseauian movements, education has ceased to be a way of forcing people to conform, and has instead pursued the ideal of being an apprenticeship undertaken with joy and pleasure. Thus, the stranglehold of the *polis* on the world of childhood has gradually loosened.

Furthermore, the development of individualism, and of the desire to live one's own life for as long as possible, has liberated parents from their children and children from their parents. The rise in the standard of living allowed the habitat to be divided up into autonomous isolated units, and children, whose rooms are equipped to receive the mass media (with magazines, record players, TV sets, radios), have been able to establish their own space in a much less supervised and much more autonomous manner than in the past. In these conditions, the combined interplay of psychic, social and economic forces has allowed for the constitution and segregation of a teen-age, then an older adolescent, age group.

American liberal education, like all forms of liberal education, had remained semi-repressive, incorporating obligations, and even punishment. It is always under semi-liberal regimes that the most virulent rebellions develop, because they allow a basic opportunity for self-expression and demonstration. In this sense, semi-liberal education allowed the rupture to happen. In fact, the rebellion has not essentially fought against the (weakened or moderate) authority of the father or of the State, but instead against the socio-cultural repression of the instincts, of childhood and adolescent aspirations. Moreover, in the process of this rebellion, adolescents have become aware of the appalling deficiencies suffered, without their knowledge, by adults who are devoted to technological and economic activism, and trapped by their petty pursuit of status and their adherence to bourgeois values. This made it possible for the identification with the father, and more broadly with adults in general, to cease to function as a socializing process. Adolescence has increasingly revealed itself in its contradictory nature as refusal or fear of the adult world, and auto-initiation into the adult world. It was possible to transform the dramatic opposition between these two terms and make them complementary when the values of children and young people were recognized as anthropological values, and when an ideal of the adult world was created that was antagonistic to the world of adults, and therefore on its way to being revolutionary.

THE THREE PATHS

I see the cultural revolution dividing into three branches: the first will disintegrate into dropping out and taking drugs; the historic junction of Ashbury and Haight streets has become a kind of Bowery for adolescents, where miserable souls with blank expressions hang around, dressed in filthy rags. And yet this is the place where the hippie revolution began, four years ago, in a rainbow of color and outlandish costume, everyone choosing his or her plumage and pelt, and singing of love and peace.

The second movement will evolve into political rebellion, either dissociating or bringing together the new urban guerilla (assassination attempts, hold-ups) and the magical hope offered by that other drug, "Marxism-Leninism."

The third movement will *perhaps* constitute an original social fabric by colonizing the neo-craft, neo-archaic sector of the economy, by making communal-cooperative experiments, by extending a solidarity network, and by transforming life-styles and interpersonal relationships.

(There will be circulation and contamination between these three movements).

Do they sense that the world is coming to an end? It's not as if they wanted to enjoy themselves before the end of the world; they want pleasure, yes, but at the same time they want to deny themselves. Everything is happening as if the end of the world had already come, as if the ruling civilization in its entirety had already been wiped out by the atomic cataclysm, and as if they were rebuilding a Crusoesque civilization out of the debris from the shipwreck.

In any case, I feel very strongly that it's *too soon, too late*.

The Sons of Champlin were playing the other night at the Matrix, a rock temple. There is something mystical and religious about their music, which achieves sublime moments in its hysteria. Each song, like a spiritual, preaches its particular message, expressing one of the great truths of the cultural revolution. There's the song *It's time to be what you are*, and another song which urges us, obsessively, enticingly:

Open the door
You can fly.

The "mansion" on Montgomery Street. A three-story house, with all its doors left unlocked. They all help each other out; in summertime they sleep on the terrace, they eat together, etc.

Of course, I'll take this further. But on leaving Frisco, I feel that my exploration is essentially over. I have visited the world I was looking for. Now I see both faces of the situation. In the beginning, I saw its sublime aspect, its marvelous vitality; now I see its misery, both subjective (felt by this revolutionized and revolutionizing youth) and objective (I mean the degradation that follows bloom, the decomposition, the dead end). I want to continue to see these two contradictory truths clearly, I want to continue to learn, but my great thirst has been quenched.

I return to San Diego with two maxims:

First maxim: you must remain marginal, which means keeping one foot in each world (because you also need a footing in the social world of work, planning for the future, and organization, if only to protect yourself from being crushed). You need *an economic basis*. ("If I tell them that, they just say *bullshit*," H. tells me). But you must *live* as much as possible in the other world, the non-bourgeois world. I feel this increasingly strongly.

Maxim number two: we need new syntheses.

STORE IN FRISCO

A boutique for pets. Just for dogs, there are toothbrushes, shampoos, collars studded with pearls or diamonds, tuxedo collars with bow ties, perfumed products to discourage suitors or ill-mannered lickers, pullovers, vests, pajamas, evening attire, little bootees or moccasins, and *Our Puppy* baby books, in which the family tree and the main events of the little dog's life are recorded, including its birthday and wedding photos.

A mynah bird in a cage suddenly pipes up in a high-pitched whistle; then he murmurs in a soft, almost plaintive little voice: *I want a pretty friend.* He whistles again, then says: *Yeah.* While we're in the shop, he calls several times for a nice little friend, and from time to time he cries *Hey pretty bird!* or *Call the doctor!*

Yes, they really need to see a doctor . . .

Another boutique just for bath stuff.

In another one, there's a fascinating gadget: two magnetic mobiles doing a courtship dance. The most extraordinary moment comes when the mobiles turn independently, each on its own side; then they decelerate imperceptibly, and their mutual attraction suddenly drags them toward each other, shuddering furiously. They never touch, but they twitch to the same rhythm, miming the act of love better than our human dances.

In another shop, a bed ripples like the sea; you can control the waves at will.

AVANT-GARDE

Life estimates that the cultural revolution has affected a large proportion of the younger generations. Millions of them are following the movement in one way or another. There are tens of thousands of civilizational activists (hippies, commune-dwellers, neo-tribalists). There are thousands of political activists (militants belonging to revolutionary organizations). Extensive common ground continues to be shared by the civilizational group and the political group; however, they are beginning to separate from each other. But what's most important is the current passing between the two poles; the essential phenomenon is still the common culture medium, in which all the little mystical and religious sects, including the Marxist-Leninist ones, are teeming like mitochondria. One wonders whether one particular sect will emerge from this lot and become *the* great religion, which is what happened two thousand years ago. Or will the victor be a strain of Marxism-Leninism again, thanks to its capacity for organization, which would enable it to combine all this aggression and this boundless hope, and channel it into disciplined and militarized action?

I'm with those who believe that the activism of the party militant is reactionary: to me, it's the existential militant who is revolutionary, it's the commune and the new network of human, social, and even economic relationships, it's the rock festival and the love-in.

Fascism or paradise: they can't see beyond this alternative; they insist on plastering these labels over the present situation. They despise liberalism, because liberalism rejects this alternative, or rather evades it, because liberalism institutes some ground rules – which they see as repression and deference, because they don't know from experience what an authoritarian and totalitarian regime is really like. To them, being expelled from

University is just as bad as, or worse than, what Sinyavsky and Daniel have suffered;[23] in their eyes at least Sinyavsky and Daniel had the advantage of living outside a capitalist regime. When I'm confronted with this attitude, I feel completely estranged from them, and closer to my friend Leslek, who sees everything he is witnessing at Berkeley in the light of his experience of popular democracy. He *knows* that the liberal status of the universities must be protected by avoiding their direct engagement in political conflict, he recognizes and senses the Stalino-Fascist seeds that are present in this movement, and are undifferentiated here from the libertarian and revolutionary seeds.

We discuss all of this, at the Lesleks' place, in Berkeley. Part of me is on his side, that's absolutely certain, but part of me takes the other side.

During this conversation, I outline to him my point of view about the succession of accident-events that have constituted the cosmos since its birth. "So," he says, "God?" "Well, no. God confirms the accidental and creational nature of the world, but does not explain it."

MITOCHONDRIA

He claims that one of his friends, a biologist, has discovered that mitochondria are gendered. What a promiscuous muddle the cell is!

CULTURE

Read a book by Cyril Dean Darlington (the English geneticist) called *The Evolution of Man and Society* (Allen and Unwin, London). Principal argument: biological evolution has not been supplanted by cultural evolution, but is currently responsible for the latter.

PAN-GENETICISM

It is clear that pioneering science here is developing a form of pangeneticism, which attempts to attribute phenomena once believed to be dependent on environment or society (culture) to hereditary factors.

We are seeing the resurgence of the notion that there is genetic inequality between individuals and between races; we can expect to see a resurgence of the theory of the intellectual superiority of the White race, especially the Aryan Anglo-Saxon-Germanic branch. They say the Judeo-Anglo-Saxon-Germanic race excels at creating industrial civilizations . . . (Nevertheless, it is singularly inept when it comes to creating a tolerable humanity . . .)

In any case, it is interbreeding and variety that allow for progress, novelty and development in all directions. Every birth breaks up and unites two foreign hereditary lots; it liberates what is virtual, performs combinations, and implements new syntheses. It is already a form of racial interbreeding. The universal interbreeding that I commended in my anthropolitics is not only a moral or cultural exigency; it is indeed the anthropo-biological norm. Honor be to mongrels like us, for we are the true representatives of the *Anthropos* . . .

Humans are still too socio-centric and ego-deficient to be capable of accepting and understanding that ethnic diversity constitutes an extraordinary panoply of wealth. They take diversity for inequality. Furthermore, scientists in developed societies are so convinced of the superiority of science, rationality and a certain type of intellectualism, that they are unable to shake off the notion that IQ measures a hierarchy of values. They never fail to distribute each particular trait on a scale of high and low, superior and inferior . . .

INTELLIGENCE

Man's intelligence is fabulously complex. It flourishes in shared, organized work in association, but still leaves ten to twenty billion neurons untapped. Even the most gifted human being makes use of only a tiny part of his or her brain. Even the least gifted human being possesses a brain whose associative capacities are sufficient for the most intelligent operations. There is no "superior brain" specific to any particular human race, and for a long time to come the brain will continue to be superior to Man himself.

Nevertheless, it is conceivable that some intellectual deficiencies or particular areas of skill depend upon very precise genetic determinants, linked for example to the deficiency or efficiency of the enzymatic reaction promoting cortical activity, which, like all enzymatization, would be governed by DNA; in other words, by the hereditary message. For this reason, we cannot rule out the notion that the chemical syntheses that are inseparable from one type or another of intellectual activity may vary according to ethnic or familial heredity.

It is also conceivable that intelligence depends on cultural determinants, and that a particular human environment, a particular education, a particular training succeeds or fails in favoring the development of certain intellectual capacities.

But *neither* should we forget that if intelligence is to flourish, it must successfully negotiate a succession of experiences in which the decisive ego-self-superego-others-group-society-environment-world dialectic is brought to bear. Accordingly, blockages or atrophies, as well as instances of hyper-agility in intelligence, may depend on accidents that have occurred within this practico-existential chain.

Therefore, we cannot conceive of intelligence as being an immediate product of either genetics or culture. Since genetics and culture are in competition or even in conflict within every human being, "cultural" intelligence is always moderated by genetics, and genetic intelligence is always moderated by culture. But we must go much further and understand that, during each person's life, experiences and accidents add their own essential moderating and determining factors.

Thus, there may be genetic, social, historical and cultural conditions that statistically favor one aspect or another of intelligence, *but above all there are intelligent individuals.* In other words, intelligence is the accidental result of a unique combination of phenomenal sequences.

And of course intelligence is not what is measured by intelligence tests. Intelligence tests are still idiotic. Intelligence is not a quality or a series of qualities, it is the conjunction of contradictory and complementary qualities, it is a polyphonic art.

THE INDIVIDUAL

Science seeks general traits. Pseudo-scientific stupidity denies the existence of individualities.

GENETIC HEREDITY, CULTURAL INHERITANCE

They combine, determining one another, rejecting one another, stifling one another, creating over-determinations, diversions and repressions, on the basis of which an individual's complex characteristics, dominant and recessive, manifest and latent, multiple and united, will be formed.

CREATING A CHEMISTRY OF IDEAS

The chemical model should help us to understand ideological combinations. Thus, in a certain combination, Puritanism (or Christianity) consolidates the established order; in another combination, it becomes revolutionary ferment.

META-MORALITY AND META-BIOLOGY

If morality is a conditioned reflex, a social simulacrum of instinct, we must seek a meta-morality. The only basis for this would be an infra-morality, or obedience to the voice of Life. Hence the necessity of reconstituting the biotic discourse so that we can recognize and listen to this voice. We have already grasped the last part of the message: humanity must take control of the biotic adventure and guide it beyond existing limits.

CHANCE

This world is condemned to chance, to living haphazardly; it is organized and structured to cope with chance. All physico-chemical attractions are designed to compensate for chance, to resist chance; the whole of biological organization is designed to deal with a world ruled by chance, that's why the genetic message has been locked up like a treasure in a coffer whose key has been thrown away, and that's why the *soma* is perishable and destined to die, and that's why there are billions and billions of seeds, spores, spermatozoa, eggs . . . but in that case what is *Chance*? Isn't it the emanation, the appearance, the sign of the first phenomenon (indetermination? accident?), on whose basis and as a reaction to which forms of *order* (in other words regularities) are constituted?

It is Chance that we should be thinking about, but it is accepted as a given by scientists, and banished by philosophers.

USA

The metabolism of this vast organism can cope with disorders that would finish off a society like France. It is even possible that this metabolism not only tolerates, but actually requires a measure of chaos and violence, in order to ensure its own survival and development. There has always been an open frontier. Could the cultural revolution be the new frontier?

American society lets off steam in these danger zones, unbridles and cultivates its fantasies; moreover, this rationalized, bureaucratized, bourgeois, prosaic, crude society draws its imaginative life and its innovating or aesthetic ferments from these zones.

All this is true of the "functional" aspect of the under-civilized, under-policed chaos . . . but to see this aspect on its own would be Crozierism. There is also a rupture and a crisis, I am sure of this.

These Anglo-Americans have been diligent and determined in their pursuit of efficiency; they lead the technicization of the planet, but they don't know how to live – and the art of living can only be learned from those whom they despise.

DDT has now been recognized as a scourge, and not a remedy . . . It infiltrates humans via plants and the animals which feed on them and which are our food. It has spread into the oceans, killing plankton, fish, and ultimately destroying all forms of life. And now it's cyclamates' turn. On the radio, on TV, in the papers, a great deal of concern has been expressed about this ersatz sweetener for dieters which is used as a sugar substitute in drinks, chewing-gum, and other sweet foods. Experiments on rats and chickens suggest that in an attempt to avoid gaining weight, and thus prevent the risk of coronary thrombosis, millions of men and women have been ingesting a carcinogen.

And so their purifier was a pollutant, their elixir was a poison.

FEEDBACK

The American machine is brutal, crude, and always primarily resorts to quantitative measures when trying to solve a problem (dollars, tons, etc.). It proceeds by trial and error, and after a time, it reacts to failure by going back and reexamining the initial plan (with more showers of dollars fuelling the inquiry). Today, as we can see with the drug and pollution problems, the feedback mechanisms don't seem to have rusted yet.

But what about Vietnam? The Black problem? Is the machine capable, not just of correcting its problem-solving devices, but of reforming itself structurally, in depth?

Otherwise, couldn't the great restructuring feedback become the new totalitarianism, if this society feels mortally threatened? Might the machine destroy its own liberal institutions in order to wipe out its internal enemies?

SCIENCE FICTION

In *Star Trek*, the TV series, the starship Enterprise comes across the god Apollo while exploring unknown galaxies. Naturally. At a certain level, all mythologies communicate with one another.

Olympus itself has been appropriated by science fiction. The Greek gods were deep space travelers who had to make a stop on Olympus, five thousand years ago, to recharge their energy. Apollo was left behind, for reasons not clearly explained, and now lives on a little planet in a temple which is an exact replica of the Parthenon.

Everything about this film seems grotesque. Apollo is an imbecile who takes the expedition's piquant blonde sociologist for Athena – although she actually looks more like a Western Airlines flight attendant. He's nostalgic for the good old Olympian days and would like to force the humans to worship him. The love scenes between Apollo and the sociologist are very silly. But despite all this (and also partly because of all this) I'm gripped by an anthropological emotion when Captain Kirk obliges the sociologist to choose between her love for the God and her human duty – and when she renounces immortality out of fidelity to the mortal race . . .

BIOS-ANTHROPOS

Man has the potential and the ability to achieve everything that has been realized in a separate, limited, and partial manner among the various living species. In this sense, he is a microcosm with respect to life. But at the same time Man is a macrocosm, which means that he is endowed, on a comparatively giant scale, with the same open-ended, indeterminate force as the miniscule original cell. It is indeed because he is a macrocosm of life as foundation that he is a microcosm of life as totality . . .

The same genius that realized (or was realized in) the wonder that is the cell can still be found in Man.

THE NEW CELL

Man: the new basic unit for fabulous nucleo-proteo-socio-noological constructions!

FERTILITY AND POLITICAL FERTILIZATION

There's no point, they say after the moratorium. What naïvete! They haven't yet realized that most political acts are pointless. Political action, like the sexual act, consists of countless utterly unproductive exertions and ejaculatory spurts of spermatozoa, of which only one may, by chance, penetrate the ovum. Militants must both believe and not believe in the need for consistency in their efforts. They must believe like the gambler who keeps betting on the lottery every week, but not like the worker for whom accumulated labor yields a finished product.

The idea that the political act is ruled by chance is unbearable to people who seek mental security.

JOHN

He believes that the young hippies' abandonment of beautiful, flamboyant costumes for miserable, dirty rags is a last resort aimed at avoiding re-assimilation by the world of consumption.

THE WAY

Once again, it's the children's crusade which is showing the way.

THE MASK OF LOVE

At San Francisco airport, we're waiting to check in when I notice an old woman with her face plastered in make-up in the line for the next counter. There's nothing extraordinary about that. In America, both aging barmaids and lady millionaires paint their faces in vivid colors as if for some archaic ceremony. But suddenly I'm fascinated when this elderly coquette puckers her lips and offers them up to a taller, well-built man; I guess he must be about forty-five years old. Their lips meet in a loving kiss and I stare, transfixed, at her rapt face. Instead of eyebrows, she has two brown lines, the color of tobacco; her eyes are skillfully made-up, and wearing long false lashes. Her skin is artificially radiant, with an impeccable blend of colors, smoothed over the bones of her face like a magnificent satin; her pretty little chin juts out oddly, as if disconnected from the rest of her face, and I can't quite work out why, but it's this chin which betrays her age. Is it because when old people have lost their teeth their chins jut out like this? But this woman has superb (false) teeth, as I see when she smiles. The shape of her mouth is concealed beneath an artificial red mouth, which is nonetheless perfectly integrated; it's a young woman's mouth, plump and sensual. I watch her as she continues to savor that delicious kiss, although the two faces have already parted. I quickly try to calculate her age, and I'm astounded to think that she could be 70, or 75. But maybe she's only 60? I can't tell; in any case this mask of love, which has just given a young girl's kiss, is making me dizzy. I weave a multitude of fantasies, in which I find myself bewitched, pursuing this creature and becoming one of her lovers, in a fabulous bed, at the heart of a palatial mansion. I imagine myself making her jealous by flirting with another aged *femme fatale*, her best friend . . . It's the same excitement I've felt when reading or watching *She*, and other films of the kind, where an eternally young and beautiful woman turns into a grotesque old crone for a few moments, before drinking her elixir of youth. And the moment that excites me is the moment of passage, that double moment when she goes from being a very young woman to a very old one, and then from very old to very young, when she is very old and very young at the same time. Yes, that's what happened. That's the mythological and devastating moment I witnessed at the airport. I didn't dare say anything to Johanne, nor to Dick, needless to say.

TAKING STOCK

What's new? Well, I'm no longer itching to immerse myself in San Francisco, or the communes, or to explore California. Now I'd rather just settle in here, after my return from Paris, and see what's going on, in the minor city of San Diego, within the field that interests me: the communes, the hippies, the cultural revolution. In any case, I'm finding out new things every day, as I get to know and master the territory.

At the same time, the nebula of my bio-anthropological reflection is thickening, swirling, but now biology and sociology are its center. I think I've found some good directions here, and that I'm focusing on the key principle. My notes are accumulating. Should I start writing soon, or should I go on with my reading, and accumulate more notes?

I'm forcing myself to go to the sea every lunchtime. The water and the air are getting colder all the time. It's torture getting into the water. But once I'm in, I feel warm.

I love diving into the wave which itself dives over me, and engulfing myself in it as it is engulfed, unfurling within it, and then getting up again, reemerging, reborn . . . Oh, and afterwards, for several hours, I feel more than good: I feel *better*.

I'm pleased with my brown body.

Something's getting on my nerves. I feel pressured, harried. But by whom, for God's sake? Nobody asks anything of me, here, only that I should be free to pursue my thoughts. But something in me panics; am I then incapable of working, of living, at a slow, calm pace? Is it the tranquility that worries me, and makes me panic? Is it because I feel that it's abnormal to experience such well-being, such freedom, that I have a premonition of some appalling catastrophe? Punishment?

LA JOLLA

Along our shores, you see a great number of birds and planes in the sky. Little tourist planes, fighter jets from the neighboring military bases performing exercises, commercial jets that have started their descent into San Diego. We hear the double boom of the fighter jets as they break the sound barrier, or we feel the house shudder, as if there'd been a little *temblor*.

Sometimes, lying on the beach, I think I see a plane through my half-open eyes, but no, it's a big bird hovering above; I open my eyes again to look at the bird, but it's a plane . . .

An injured gray pelican crash-landed on the beach the other day.

There's a lovely drive over the crest of the hill, along a line of dunes, between the Salk and the sea. High cliffs from which you look down at the deserted beaches and the rushing waves.

Tour (of the outside) of the Salk again with Touraine, on Sunday. Dusk. We're struck by the beauty of this building. From the east, facing the land, the road, and the social "world," it's a closed blockhouse; from the west, it opens with all its windows onto the Ocean and the Cosmos. Touraine has the impression that the entire building is braced and ready, scrutinizing the horizon of the future. Later Jonas tells us that rather than having his Institute face east, like a temple, he wanted it to face the setting sun (because of Minerva's bird? I can't remember the reason he gave me).

Weekend with Touraine and the Kolakovskis.

The Zoo. The coyotes are incredible little fellows, like bourgeois from the reign of Louis-Philippe. The old Socratic bison meditate.

Seeing the diversity of species, the astonishing combinations, the play of colors, the stripes, the spots, etc., you get a strong impression that *life is amusing itself* (to keep from crying).

Discovered the fish restaurant on Marinas.

On La Jolla Boulevard, a guide-car announces a "special cargo."

Indeed: taking up all three lanes, a house rolls by, borne on a trailer. Sweet young girls. They're killing flies.

Although smoking a single cigarette makes me feel terrible, and upsets my whole metabolism, I'm going through a phase where when I'm working I sometimes feel the irrepressible urge to light one up: desire for a hot breath in my mouth, for a mouth to mouth.

CRISIS

Elements for my *crisis sociology*: medicine has made its progress thanks to pathology: experiments create pathological conditions so that systems, pushed to their limits, reveal what they conceal under normal conditions: their fundamental mechanisms and their possibilities.

JONAS

Dinner the night before last with Jonas. Although he's more optimistic, my ideas and his resonate on every point.

He tells me that in Chinese, the ideogram for the word "crisis" forms the junction between the one meaning danger and the one meaning opportunity.

He takes his bearings from the *self*, *me*, *I* triad. (Self: the *germen*, the *phylum*; Me, the *soma*, the body; I, the junction of the two within the subject). He believes that "God" is in the Self.

And it occurs to me, at that moment, that God is the projection of the genetic, of the unknown genius that is *within* man.

There is a genius somewhere . . .

BLINDNESS

The wonder that is the eye only allows us to perceive a minute selection of frequencies and sequences. It is a tiny breach in our blindness.

SOCIETY

Is society a blind creature? An animal without eyes, without senses? A living being possessing a central system, reflexes, feedback, servo-mechanism, etc. What is this *weird creature* which is neither a machine nor an animal?

CHAOS

Chaos, according to Plato, is limitless, formless, meaningless, without direction; in fact it doesn't even exist (Véro's letter).

JAKOBSON

Read Roman Jakobson's fascinating *Linguistics in Relation to Other Sciences* (Speech for the Twentieth Congress of Linguistics in Bucharest, to be published in *UNESCO, New Trends in Social Research*). Now I'm finally convinced that there is a biology-language-society axis.

(Parenthesis: he writes that, in linguistics, "the opposition between the diachronic and the synchronic is collapsing at every point." And yet it remains pompously triumphant in the provinces colonized by structural linguistics).

INVENTION

Jonas Salk tells me to read *The Structure of Scientific Revolutions* by Thomas Kuhn, which shows that eccentrics and outsiders are responsible for inventions.

In *The False Images of Science*, Gerald Holton warns that the marginal, unorthodox individual must be protected: "We must keep a special place for him and protect him – if only to symbolize our commitment to science itself rather than to a new machinery."

Jakobson (in *op. cit.*), "Indefiniteness and creative power appear to be entirely interrelated."

And also: "Natural language (as opposed to formal languages) provides the medium for invention, imagination, and creativity."

THE YOUTH REVOLUTION

I arrived here when the hippie phenomenon was beginning to be repressed, and entering its decline. Its golden age was '66–'67.

At first sight, this decline seems to be an internal phenomenon: a result of the damage done by drugs. But the damage done by drugs is, up to a point, a result of the repression, and especially of the *cordon sanitaire* that has been imposed.

So instead of following its own course, the movement has been diverted, has diverted.

Still, some extraordinary things remain, and something is still happening. The ground swell itself is growing stronger all the time, and sweeping up adolescents aged around 14 or 15.

This is an event in the history of humanity.

It's an eruption, a mutation, which is almost (why almost?) biological. A variant of the *anthropos* is being born, but it's too weak, it's going to die, they've murdered it, it's weeping . . .

That is why they are so sad. They know that they are being murdered.

I must be a witness, not a voyeur.

Friendship and love: these are my substitutes for hippieism; these, along with the search for truth, are what we must keep or place at the center of our lives.

I'm going to study how the crisis of adolescence is coinciding with the crisis of society and the crisis of humanity.

From my perspective here, I see very clearly that the fire at the heart of May 1968 was the cultural revolution, and not a baptismal ceremony for the new Tourainian or Malletist class. (Incidentally, bold print on the cover of Serge Mallet's book reads: "The new working class, spearhead of May 1968"; just one year after he's completely *forgotten* that the "spearhead" was the students).

ANIMAL FRIENDSHIP

I've already written that the new culture in its entirety was contained, in embryonic form, within the culture of childhood (the Mowgli myths, animals who talk to humans, noble sentiments, etc.). Once again, progress must take the form of the childhood world surfacing in adult life.

You often see young people here with German shepherd dogs. They treat these animals as friends, rather than training them to be guard dogs, and the dogs bound around joyfully, lark about on the beach, or walk quietly beside their masters (is master the right word in this case?) These German shepherds are not at all aggressive, they are gentle and calm. One more proof of the strange symbiosis between dogs and humans. The students take their dogs on campus with them. Dogs attend Marcuse's lectures, patient and apparently attentive.

BREAKING AWAY

Van, the leather craftsman on 5th Street, has a stall where he makes belts and sandals on his workbench, in front of his customers; he was a businessman until he quit his lucrative profession. He's happy; he's grown a beard. He's a volunteer delivering the free press to the psychedelic shops, and introduces the kids to Mary-Jane.

My brothers are those who sense the grimness of careers in business and management, etc.

THE ADOLESCENT AND SOCIAL CLASS

These bourgeois kids have made a desperate attempt to escape from the bourgeoisie (and now I'm closer to understanding why they cling to the myth of the proletariat as dispenser of justice, and brutal destroyer: it's precisely because they want to liberate themselves).

In a different way, the youngsters who form antisocial gangs in the ghettoes are making their own desperate attempt to escape from the class of white-collar workers or from the proletariat. It's extraordinary to see how modern adolescents are rejecting social class, in favor of either a national definition (young Blacks, young Indians) or an anthropological definition.

AMERICA

Yes, I think I've seen my theory confirmed: the place where the bourgeois, bureaucratic, capitalist civilization is most advanced will be the breeding ground for the real revolution.

The orbiting Apollo X astronauts look down upon America, and recognize Los Angeles by its atmospheric sewer of brown smog, spewed by four million cars, which have spread a blanket of unconsumed hydrocarbons, tetraethylic lead and carcinogenic nickel additives over the city.

Tobacco causes cancer, and heart disease. It's legal. Marijuana is harmless, and it is illegal. Harmless? Yes and no: because marijuana promotes an experience which radically contradicts the entire value system of activity and effort upon which western society is based; tobacco, on the other hand, destroys human beings without corrupting the social structures. The prohibition of marijuana is sociologically understandable. (But of course it would be possible to integrate marijuana; in the juvenile-hippie context marijuana is revolutionary, but it could be integrated in another context where its function would change: in Vietnam, for example, all the front line soldiers smoke, because marijuana makes you forget). It could be integrated in the same way as alcohol.

The cigarette ads on TV brush away the specter of cancer by flourishing images of clean air, nature, water, sky, vigor.

WE CAN FLY

On Saturday, there's a pot party at Z.'s place. The good combination of grass, tequila, Mexican food and dancing frees me of all my anxiety; this is euphoria to me: a natural state, but one that is perpetually thwarted by continual anxiety, which takes many forms: haste, impatience, concern, worry, remorse, etc. And now here I am, by this grace, brought back to my natural state, in the Rousseauian sense; to my innocence. Every now and then I taste the full lips of two or three American women, and here again my constantly inhibited natural desire is expressing itself; just as dogs excitedly sniff at passing strangers of their species, so my instinctive inclination is to taste the lips of women I meet or merely pass in the street. A constant micro-repression prevents me from doing so, and I'm not even sure whether this micro-repression isn't worse than the big one, which imposes itself upon me with the intransigent force of a quasi-instinct.

Yes, I was deliciously content: I felt neither depression nor bliss, not even happiness or euphoria, but something more primitive which was like the common root of all those feelings and which powerfully contained them as if under glass. Although it usually worries me to see Johanne descending into the realm of alcohol, this time I was untroubled. Our return home was beautiful. At two in the morning, we all wrapped up warm, and sped off in the Mini-Moke, open to the winds, down Interstate 5. "We're flying, we're flying!" we yelled at each other, ecstatically. *Yeah! We can fly!*

E.S.P. Extra-sensory perception (pot's gift to its blessed smokers).

TIJUANA

Yesterday, Sunday, incredible emotion at the Tijuana bullring, where El Cordobes was performing; the crowd booed him at first, but he made them respect him.

Tijuana, a bazaar of a town, a brothel-town, a Pigalle for Americans. Surrounding it, the shanty towns where all the people who set off from the depths of Mexico to cross the dollar's border, and who were turned away, are camping out, waiting.

Although this is an artificial town, its need for money is real, and that's why it sells itself for gringo dollars. And after all, it remains Mexican. In the streets of Tijuana, Johanne feels at ease, and so do I. These brown skins, these Latino-Indian faces are oxygen to us.

PARTY

Janis, a gorgeous fifty-year old, fascinated both Johanne and me. But there was a little spermatozoidal lover clambering about all over her (a little Jewish photographer, who turned out to be very nice).

LOBSTER

Went back the other day to the fresh fish café, with its homely atmosphere, in a lovely spot on Mission Bay, between Pacific and Ocean Beach. We ate our lobster facing the fishing boats.

SAN DIEGO

I'm beginning to love San Diego. This amorphous extent of land, this center-less urban sprawl is revealing a few of its nuclei, a few of its mitochondria to us. I feel like I'm inside an enormous protoplasm.

THE VAULTED SKY

Just as in a cathedral the organ makes you aware of and accentuates the majestic height of the nave, so here the organ-like drone of the jet planes, very high up and calm, makes you aware of the grandiose immensity of this marine sky.

AGONY

A weird guy, a very American kind of giant, like a jovial gorilla, wearing a white jacket with "cobra" written on it, and a color drawing of a green cobra on a red background, comes up to us near the Coves, cackling dementedly. He starts asking us questions, and at first I think he's very drunk, but it gradually becomes clear that it's something else, he's tripping, what on? LSD? He hands me two business cards with his name on them, but on one he's a real estate agent, and on the other he sells cars. He tells us that his mother, a French-Canadian, was born in Trois-Rivières, but that as a little boy he swore to her never to speak French. Why? His expression becomes mysterious.

"Perhaps you can start speaking French now," I say. "No," he replies, earnest in the extreme.

He says to Johanne, and this is the extraordinary part: "I'm going to tell you my name, and you'll understand because you're a woman . . . My name is agony."

LOYS

Just now, while flicking through *Le Monde*, I found out that Loys Masson has died. A wave of shock and distress ran through me. A fraternal bond developed between us when the same immunological reaction made us both rebel against chauvino-Jdanovism.[24] That was a long time ago, more than twenty years, and we hardly ever saw each other again afterwards. We had been united in and against the Party, and our divorce from the Party separated us. And now here I am left facing this dead man, holding a stalk of friendship in my hand . . .

Then, as I was mulling over all these thoughts on leaving the Salk, another, utterly different, feeling suddenly emerged into consciousness: it was the feeling that had gripped me the instant I read the announcement of Loys Masson's death, before my sadness had seized the opportunity to push it back down again into the depths: relief. "It's him, and it's not me . . . " How shameful . . . But I peer down further into the depths again, and discover that shame is not the right word, because I knew I had this feeling, but I did not express it, I stored it away in the subconscious, and so I realize that whenever I read the paper or listen to the news, I'm just waiting for a dead person to devour who is not myself. Not just any old dead person, but a dead person I know, a close dead person, a dead friend.

BIOS

I have a feeling that after Man, on the basis of Man, life would like to try its hand at something else . . . .

But why this obstruction, this infirmity, in a power that otherwise possesses such fertile vigor? What sickness is genius suffering from? What blindness? What is keeping it prisoner?

CHEMISTRY

Yes, yes, it's all there already in the molecules!

Attraction, repulsion, combination, structure building, explosion and combustion have become our selves, our loves and our hates . . .

I like the fact that love springs from chemical affinity.

LABORIT

I'm re-reading *Biologie et Structure* here. It's a badly constructed book, disorganized and repetitive; but what a torrent of ideas, forging ahead over rivers and mountains as he makes the journey from the biological entity to the social entity.

Among other notes I've taken (and which I'll quote from elsewhere), there are some excellent passages on multidisciplinarity (p. 152) and on research (p. 144).

PAIN

Laborit defines pain as being that which expresses (or accompanies) a stable increase in the cellular metabolism caused by a depolarization; this increase is aimed at reestablishing the potential of the primitive membrane. Therefore, and I find this conclusion striking, "pain is a general phenomenon, common to all living structures."

PROGRESS

"It is in periods of instability that each society and each individual is capable of making progress" (Laborit, p. 68). Yes, progress requires and creates instability. But at the same time it represents a mortal danger. And instability can result in regression and catastrophe. The word progress is ontologically, philosophically, biologically and historically linked to its opposite. Thus, we can appreciate the wisdom of conservatism. As well as its stupidity.

Laborit also says, more or less, that progress will come neither from the West nor the East, nor from the Third World, but from the *globalization of humanity*.

"Tomorrow's world will belong to the Utopians" (Laborit, p. 85). I'd add: and not to the technocrats.

POLITICAL DIALECTICS

Once we realize that our every action engenders a reaction; once we know that we can more or less predict the direction, force, and form of this reaction, then, when we want to achieve a particular goal, we should not only aim to one side of the target, away from it, just as when shooting at a moving target one must move oneself, but we should also envisage our action in terms of the art of billiards, where the ball being aimed at is never the target; rather, it plays an instrumental role in a series of actions and reactions, and only their final outcome is supposed to attain the desired result.

Moreover, this world is not governed by ballistics, and political action (when its aim is innovation, provoking evolution or revolution) scans uncharted terrain for a synthesis whose concrete properties can only be very partially guessed at. Hence:

1. The terrific risk of any action undertaken in the desire and belief that it will be progressive, and the often greater progressive role of actions that started out being reactionary and *which have unleashed the progressive counter-forces*. It seems that progress has more often unleashed reactions, and that reactions have more often unleashed progress.

2. The necessary Machiavellism which efficiency would lead us to adopt . . .

Or rather even this:

We should be conscious of the fact that one party potentially and sometimes actually scores points for the opposing party (in this light the Stalinist notion that Leftism is potentially right-wing is not absurd in principle, but it should be complemented by the notion that Stalinism is potentially, and as we know today, actually anti-socialist). In the same way, it is clear that in politics we unintentionally make "provocations," which unleash the effects most contrary to our initial intention.

Conclusion: political analysis should be complex, and should detect and foresee all the counter-agents that will be activated by the agents; and above all: *the art of politics must be ingenious*.

RIVALRY, COMPETITION, FREEDOM

Note that the world of rivalry is, whether simultaneously or alternately, a world of the jungle, of regulation (the democratic, liberal interplay of parties), and of freedom (of the press, information, science). What does our dream of a non-competitive world signify? Should we not restrict ourselves to hoping only for islands of non-competition? (I'll look at all this again from another angle, that of the relationship between biology and economics).

ME

My mobility (not only mental, but geographic) allows me to de-center myself, re-center myself, helps me avoid confining myself to one or two obsessions.

ANTHROPOLOGY OF DEATH

According to Jakobson, Man is defined by tool use, language, and the incest taboo (in other words, for him, as for Lévi-Strauss, by exchange). He too, like the others, forgets about death, by which I mean the specifically human attitudes regarding the corpse, the ritual of funerals, beliefs in survival or rebirth.

Death is the anthropological breach at the heart of the relationship between individual and species.

But just as there is something fundamentally biotic, anterior to Man, in language, isn't there also something anterior to Man in his ontological refusal and mythological negation of death? Doesn't life, in which the death of individuals and the will to live of the species are closely intermingled, make apparent in Man its own contradiction, its own despair, its own illusion? (All this for the new preface to *L'Homme et la mort*).

SOCIOLOGY

I'm gleaning, here and there, quite a few elements for my sociological themes. (Why on earth can't I manage to find a unifying concept for this sociology – which has got to be: 1. historical, 2. factual, 3. related to situations of crisis?).

Salk: "It is in abnormal circumstances that we can know what a living creature is, for that is when it reveals its possibilities."

K. Mannheim: "The approach *in statu nascendi* is the closest to the experimental attitude, as opposed to the post mortem approach" (*Man and Society in An Age of Reconstruction*, Harcourt Brace, New York, p. 189).

J.-P. Aron: "The problem is not so much defining the vital structures, as defining the passage from structures to other structures" (*Essais d'épistemologie biologique*, p. 73).

Lamarck sensed the importance of circumstances (which I will call the event, the accident) "absolute power, greater even than nature . . . , the capacity of circumstances to modify all of nature's processes" (*Système analytique des connaissances positives de l'homme*, Paris, 1820, pp. 42–43; quoted by J.-P. Aron).

THE FREE PRESS COMMUNE

Yesterday, I made my first visit to the Free Press Commune in San Diego, with Bob and Pamela Mang.

For four months now, twenty of them, girls and boys, with one child, have been living in a compound of three houses with garages (converted into living-quarters), sharing everything, and adhering to W. Reich's principles of sexual freedom. This living community is also a work community; they produce the newspaper, and have also embarked upon other economic activities: the girls have started doing neo-craft work (sewing, leather, jewelry) and, in the next few days, the commune will open a shop to distribute all these products; it will also be a coffee shop and meeting place. In the coming months, a communal colony will devote itself to agriculture. The community has its own mechanical repair shop for motorbikes, cars and the bus that takes the twenty members of the "family" to parties or demonstrations. The commune's political activity is continuous, with the newspaper, plus a special supplement for marines, *The Free Duck* (San Diego is the principal naval base for ships bound for Vietnam). So the commune is multidimensional: it is anchored in a particular way of life, fights on the political front, and is well-established on a diversified economic basis, which ensures its survival but also allows for expansion. Members are aged between twenty and thirty; the initiators are students who quit the University: they gave up their careers, and they also tired of student agitation, and decided to be militant in a more committed way within their own lives, a way in which their whole selves were more powerfully engaged. First they set up the newspaper, then they founded the commune. They have also created their own micro-society: democracy in work, fraternity in life. Their initial intention was not only to find an oasis, but to build a platform of influence and action; their aim is combat rather than mere survival. They set out to succeed, success being defined not as the discovery of a permanent formula, but the ability to cope with the successive problems they will face.

Johanne and I talked most of all to Jan, a twenty-seven-year-old from Holland, one of this commune's pioneers. He says that for the first time he's found the kind of life that suits him. And we marvel as we discover more about this initiative, which is as bold as it is well thought-out. I believe, as they do, that revolutionary problems are being tackled at their root here.

We had dinner in the dining room, sitting on mats, at low tables made of long planks, Japanese style. They take turns to cook. The provisions come from welfare and God knows what other crafty schemes. Everyone helps himself. There's a big pot of brown rice, another of meatballs in Mexican sauce, another of fruit in syrup. Their faces are relaxed and serene. Jan says that the commune refuses to take on people who are too young, or who have too many problems; this is not a healing center. Newcomers are adopted after a general discussion, but if just one member vetoes an aspirant, he or she will be turned down.

We visit the bedroom-cum-workshops. They each have their own room, and although the beds are all unmade, every room has an attractive, decorated look about it and appears to be clean. A lot of posters, quite a few of Che, Eldridge Cleaver, Vietnamese fighters, etc.

Here again you can see that the American cultural revolution has no hero of its own, and cobbles together its pantheon out of fighters against and martyrs to imperialism. There's a curious ambivalence with regard to Marxism. These pioneers know that Marx, Lenin and Mao have not provided the formulae for their revolution, and perhaps not even for *the* revolution, but they see them as wise guardians of the macro-social part of Truth. They see Marxism as a distant treasure to which they have not yet had access. They don't know that their strength lies in their ignorance of orthodox Marxism. They even feel a little ashamed of being "politically" ignorant, as if a pre-constituted political science existed for them to learn.

I'd like to come back to this commune, not just as a visitor, but as a witness, and stay for a while, watch it live; I'd even like to make a study of it. An article? Or go deeper? Get them to cooperate with me on a monograph?

They have correctly identified the economic sectors to be occupied and colonized. And for my part, I see more clearly and more broadly the possibilities that are objectively on offer to the commune movement: not only neo-craft work, and paleo-agriculture, but also an entire "tertiary" sector: cafés, cultural activities, journalism, publishing (they're planning to publish Reich's book on the mass-psychology of Fascism). So this is a form of neo-kibbutzism, which, unlike the Zionist kibbutz, does not precede the industrial and capitalist economies, but succeeds them. These are the uncertain, ephemeral and necessarily limited roots of a cultural revolution, for communes are the only means of existing and developing within, alongside and against the capitalist economy. And this economic basis is the only one to allow new ways of living to be tried out.

I suggest to Jan that they could already try exchanging information and experiences between the different communes; they should begin with a special column in their newspaper; they should even start thinking right now about a great federation, which would not be centrally organized, but would instead be a kind of switchboard. I'm already daydreaming about the first worldwide congress of communes.

FUTURE

I feel incapable of foresight . . . So many new seeds . . . Will they be crushed? Are these merely forerunners, heralding the possibility of a new era, or are they truly the beginnings of a new era? Looking at the demographic, economic, political, and mythological turn that things are taking in the world, I feel that we are almost inevitably headed for more upheavals and for new forms of tyranny.

My only hope: an event!

This human clay is so raw that it could be pulled in any direction. So many enzymes are at work in it. In any case, it will be changed. Who will change it? It's true that a massive infiltration is possible here.

CZECHOSLOVAKIA AND VIETNAM

Implicit, perverse but logical conclusion that I draw from the excellent article, signed "X," about Czechoslovakia in *Le Monde*. The author deplores the fact that this country remains a prisoner while Vietnam is liberating itself. In other words: the Vietnamese are in the process of liberating themselves in order to establish the very regime from which the Czechs wish they could liberate themselves.

POLITICAL ECOLOGY

In the text that Mang passed on to me ("Values, Process and Forms," by Ian L. Mc Harg (*Second International Symposium of the Smithsonian Institution, the Quality of Man's Environment*, Washington D.C., February 1967), there's another critique of political economy, coming this time from biological ecology. The present economic system cannot account for, embrace, or translate the value of the sun, the source of all life; nor that of the moon, the stars, the seasons, the physical processes, the life-forms, their roles, their symbiotic relationships, or common genetic resources. Thus the most important things have no value or rather are "priceless" from the perspective of political economy.

It's clear that the mercantile-capitalist principle of value is under attack here. This is a crucial element of the great cultural revolution: economic value is being attacked by other values which were once its neighbors, and which are firmly established within Western civilization: the ethical, aesthetic, religious, philosophical, Greco-Judeo-Christian values. (And we have witnessed entire sections of Christianity detaching themselves from the bourgeois-capitalist world in the West, in Latin America, in order suddenly to oppose it). But the new political ecology also contains something different, which Mc Harg's text clearly conveys: a pantheistic feeling for nature, whereby man has ceased to claim to be the sovereign master of the cosmos, choosing instead to make himself the obedient son and heir of life. This is the new bio-humanist ethic, whose emergence is linked to that of the new political ecology.

The latter is a descendant of the neo-Rousseauism I mentioned earlier, and its appearance is a direct result of the increasingly serious threat posed by worldwide environmental pollution. Political ecology wants to return to and re-establish the symbiosis between Man and Life, and take it one stage further. In these circumstances, ecology has become a linchpin science: it is the science that examines the organic dialectic of relationships, no longer between Man and his environment, which is a flat notion, but between Man and the other systems; it is also the science that studies the fragile super-systems constituted in such conditions. It is, at the same time, the science of modulations.

Thus, ecology is at the crossroads of a multidimensional and dialectical science on the one hand, and a new pan-biological philosophy-religion on the other.

CALIFORNIA! CALIFORNIA!

This is the crest of the wave of Western civilization, caught at the moment when it is turning back on itself and is perhaps about to topple over. After hippieism, and extending it, the crop of communes has sprung up, and now they are rejecting the ultimate pillar, the very foundation of all social organization, namely the family, in order to create, to search for, a new type of family based on affinity, free choice, love, and community. For the first time, a new way of life, a new potential structure, will be tried out, and it will no longer be restricted to a few isolated, visionary, or marginal individuals, but will be the major experience of the avant-garde of an entire generation. Of course, this is just the first stage, which can only result in failure, and there will be more and more failures, some because of an excessively rigid, dogmatic, doctrinaire commune-ism, others because of carelessness and the inability to ensure and accept regulation. But this is only the beginning of the movement's history; in the same way, it took several centuries before the medieval communal movement, which emerged at the height of the feudal era, could break free and achieve its own mode of organization, generating cities and with them the bourgeoisie, and fostering the new civilization. Today, in this place, at the heart of the most advanced form of bourgeois civilization, and generated by personal experience of its deficiencies, we can see the first outline of a post-bourgeois civilization. What spontaneity, what violence, what candor underlie this rejection, this quest!

Whereas in France the movement is primarily ideological and political, the American movement is existential and aims at revolutionizing the way we live. Whereas in France the revolutionary corpus is pre-constituted, armor-plated, and utterly impervious to other influences, in accordance with its species, which is to say a highly orthodox variant of Marxism-Leninism, here the sustaining elements have come swarming from every corner of the planet, and have united in response to a great need which aspires to self-recognition; however, although these elements are present, they are either disconnected, merely existing alongside one another, or else they are heaped together in a great syncretized mish-mash: fragments of Far-Eastern wisdom, pollen gleaned from Hinduism or Zen, primitive Christianity (and primitive communism), intuition of the Indian's archaic truths, unorthordox Fourierism, vulgar Marxism, embryos of a pan-cosmic religion of love . . . What catalyst, what enzyme could bring all of them together, and use them to fashion the new religion, the new communism . . . ?

Of course, it's possible that none of this will come to anything; the global crisis, and especially that of the United States, makes regressive eventualities more than likely, and all these seeds will be pitilessly crushed before they can pass on the life within them. On the other hand, vulgar Marxism could end up stifling the other seeds and imposing its stranglehold here as well . . .

Global innocence is the saving grace of the Californian movement. Global ignorance will be its downfall . . .

CALIFORNIA! CALIFORNIA! 2

Here we are at the heart of the chaos from which love and violence spring.

CALIFORNIA! CALIFORNIA! 3

It is here that western society has begun the process of total mutation:

1. Technological mutation, and at a deeper level, biological revolution;

2. The youth revolution, which is pregnant with a new civilization, and a new religion, but could also abort in decomposition or regression;

3. At the same time, the gestation of a new authoritarian, hierarchical, community-based order, which would destroy the premises of the youth revolution,[25] wipe out what has been accomplished by a very old liberal constitution, and would, furthermore, be able to take advantage of the opportunities offered by the techno-scientific revolution.

But all of this will be thwarted by the action and the dialectical interaction of chaos on a global scale. The different future destinies of the USSR, China, the Third World and Europe will push all the current processes off course, or even pervert them, and it may turn out to be the greatest abortion in all of human history – it would be too presumptuous to say in the history of the galaxy. (We will never know what abortions the planet and the cosmos have already been through . . .).

BIOS

Each of us, when we are born, has already relived in nine months the entire history of life in the sea and on the earth. And our cerebral cortex knows nothing about it. We have no consciousness, no memory of it . . . But what damned partition is cutting us in two? Why this iron curtain in my own house? Why is my brain, with all its millions of neurons, incapable of deciphering my being? Why can't it read in my sperm the amazing story that is written there? Will we find a way, one day, of making something talk to us, and sing, if only a sperm? An egg?

COOPERATION

Our body consists of thirty billion cells, cooperating within the integrated system that constitutes our individuality. It's a society with twelve times more members than the planet has human beings . . . And still we doubt that a global society is possible?

EVOLUTION

Why couldn't another branch of life, insects or mammals, evolve in the direction of language and intelligence?

Our time is too short, and we behave as if the evolution of all the species was complete, apart from our own . . .

When will we know whether or not Man is a failure?

TIME

At one extreme, there is the time a reaction takes, or a cellular multiplication: an infinite fraction of a second. At the other, the millions of years nebulae take to develop . . . And here we stand, bewildered, between those micro-times and these macro-times whose existence we are discovering . . .

Does time measure irreversibility, or is it the latter that measures time? (Is what I've just written interesting or idiotic?)

INFORMATION

Turn information into meaning. We do it too much, and not enough.

INVISIBLE

We can never see what is invisible, and which is the real agent, the subject, what lives, but we can always see the signs of its presence, its underpinnings, its phenomenal trace. We can track down the invisible by observing the visible. To speculate, to see, is to be blind to the invisible, and yet at the same time to see its traces (gibberish).

WHAT I'VE BEEN READING

John Stuart Mill: "Suppose that all your objects in life were realized, that all the changes in institutions and opinions which you are looking forward to could be completely effected at this very instant. Would this be a great joy and happiness to you? And an irrepressible self-consciousness answered, 'No!' At this, my heart sank within me: the whole foundation on which my life was built fell down" (quoted in "Education and the Technological Society," by John Schaar and Sheldon S. Wolin, *New York Review of Books*, 9 November 1969). This article is a brilliant exploration of the new crisis in techno-scientific knowledge, whose result will be intellectual fragmentation. The trend is toward "privatization" rather than sharing knowledge and experience. This is a double "privatization." On the one hand, knowledge becomes the professional property of the scientist, researcher, academic, technician or specialist; on the other, values, now that they are no longer linked to a theory or to a shared branch of knowledge, become their private harvest of needs and personal experience. "It is the nature of techno-scientific culture to privatize values and to render them unshareable." The authors' very astute diagnosis, which applies to the highest-ranking of academics, is that "a closer look reveals weakness beneath professionalization, atomization beneath organization, powerlessness beneath power."

Splendid conclusion: *"The great intellectual task of the present is the task of rethinking every aspect of technological civilization. That this civilization inherently moves toward self-destruction is now clear, and any radical rethinking must start from the premise that its manifest destructiveness will not be stopped by a broader distribution of the values or a more intensive application of the methods and process which constitute and sustain the evil itself. If the Universities want to dedicate themselves to this rethinking, then they would not only serve society in the most valuable way possible, but they might even save themselves."*

SALVATION AND LOSS

These "antisocial" young people: hippies, revolutionaries, and rebels who are a menace to society, will be its saviors, since it is through them that society will become conscious of its flaws, its deficiencies, and its needs; in other words, of the illness it was harboring in secret. Society will kill them, and will then be able to assimilate the results of the experiment in tranquility.

THINGS TO REFLECT UPON AND WRITE ABOUT

I've made a rough classification of my accumulated notes under the following headings:

Physis.

Bio-cosmology.

Bios.

Chance.
Logo-biology and language (separately and together).
Bio-sociology.
Anthropo-biology.
Bio-politics.
Bio-morals.
Brain.
And a few notes on "sound thinking."

Tomorrow I'm leaving for Europe.

November
PARIS

Things that were left to fend for themselves are deteriorating, falling apart. The car has forgotten how to start, although its battery isn't flat; the gas heating takes at least ten minutes to shake off its torpor; the apartment is filthy, dusty. Dust, symbol of universal entropy. Life is what puts things back in order, gets them moving, blows away the dust.

Me too, I have to get things moving, or rather free what has been held up. The divorce has been held up, for example, because I didn't acknowledge receipt of summons to the conciliation procedure. I have to wander through the labyrinth of the Palais de Justice, and disturb a stuffed shirt in the interview room, who then goes to work himself disturbing books, files and papers, finds nothing, come back tomorrow, etc.

Paris is rainy, Paris is gray. In Paris: comet-like meeting (with J.), friends, M.'s face, CNRS (French National Research Center), CECMAS, seminar, students, *Rumor in Orleans*.[26]

Evening of the 17th: Orléans, discussion about the rumor at the Cultural Center.

Paris: what possessed me to start licking F.'s boots? I bump into him in front of the Seuil office. I praise his magazine (which I have never read) to the skies. We exchange coquetries, I started it. We part company like two old whores. Why? I think I know. Sometimes, I feel that I have too many enemies, and that I've made these enemies myself through my own negligence and indifference, and so I hastily pay a literary compliment.

"Huh! It's not modern" (non-Althusserian Marxism, non-Lacanian psychoanalysis, etc.). This seculo-centrism is just as stupid as ethnocentrism. It rejects as being old-fashioned, obsolete, erroneous, condemned, everything that does not fit the canons of modernity. It's an ambitious and ridiculous attempt to monopolize the modern, in order to take possession of that majestic point which affords a panoramic view of time, for one or two seconds.

Lunch with Jacques Monod. He thinks that the whole thing was, still is, a game of quantal roulette. The birth and the evolution of life are children of chance. Chance! Chance! (I'll come back to this).

He says of B. : "He has no soul." I say: "He doesn't want to save humanity." And I think, although I know that it's *very dangerous*: "It's vital to want to save humanity."

BERGNEUSTADT

In a basin surrounded by piney hills, a forested region which looks wild, but which is in fact already teeming with factories (it's right next to the Ruhr valley), stands the Fritz Ebert Foundation, a social-democratic cultural center, which is almost brand new, and looks something like a cross between a sanatorium, a college and a housing project. It's here that, for four days, on a mountain more social-democratized than magic, twenty or thirty of us are cloistered together for a conference on violence. Ecstasies of both mind and palate are lacking (ugh, that sweet Rhine wine) but in the end I find it interesting, because when I was confronted with this notion of violence, I realized that it has never been a fundamental or operative concept for me, and that in fact I was right: because the notion of violence conceals heterogeneities rather than revealing what they have in common.

During the sessions of this conference held by the International Association for the Freedom of Culture, the lines of force and division begin to reveal themselves. On one side are the former revolutionaries, Communists or Trotskyists, who have become allergic to the tiniest dose of revolutionism, their radar detecting the distant heralds of Stalinist arrogance and terror in every instance of verbal excess or intellectual over-excitement. On the other side are the new revolutionaries, student representatives, and young semi-students of the New Left, who sense and who know that the old Left, the ex-revolutionaries, are now comfortably installed within the establishment, and who see the liberalism and the skepticism of the old guard as an incontestable proof of their corruption. And then there's the third cohort, the flabby protoplasm, the academics, technicians and specialists who have more or less tested the political waters with the tips of their toes, and who must be utterly bewildered by the whole business. And I think to myself (and write down): "I'm one of the old fools, an ex-Communist, and at the same time I'm one of the young fools, a new Communist. As for the other fools, I don't understand them at all and they don't understand me either."

"The question is: 'Socialism or Barbarism'?" cries an American student.

"And what about barbaric socialism?" retorts Melvin Laski, sarcastically.

"Did you hear that?" people ask each other indignantly, in the corridor afterwards. But I think the counter-question was as valid as the question. Either what has happened and is still happening in the USSR is the first horrible and barbaric phase in a new civilization, or else it is a monstrous failure, an avatar of Asiatic tyranny, which we must reject in order to start afresh on a new basis. There are two corresponding political sides, depending on the way in which you answer the question. But what answer would I give?

Hamilton: three differentiated effects of violence (which may be cumulative) on the Blacks: 1. radicalization, 2. politicization, 3. traumatization.

Steiner: his only tonic is the deepest pessimism. "God doesn't give a damn about us," he declares, with a happy chuckle.

STRASBOURG

Strasbourg, conference at the FLEC (Liberation Front of the Enclave of Cabinda): "Can the human sciences replace the humanities?" Three situationists try to heckle me (since 1962, the situationists have being trying to throw me into the trashcan of history, being ignorant of the fact that I've been in there for ages already, and so have they). Rescued by the director of the FLEC. This little, wiry, dried-out old Alsacien, wearing a black frock-coat, marches up to the hecklers in the back row, who are ready to take on all the policemen in the world, but who suddenly take to their heels when the little old man in the frock-coat yells at them: "Do you want me to kick your ass?" At the end, I'm subjected to a tedious ritual of questions from the ever-vigilant Maoists and Stalinists who have been mobilized onto this particular sector of the ideological front; as for the academics, they listen to me with polite boredom; I've tried to express what I think is essential, but I'm not on the same wavelength as either of the factions, we don't sense or conceive of the same problems. God I'm bored. I understand more clearly than ever that it's not my role to teach, nor to speak at conferences, but to write for isolated individuals.

Return in the sleeping car that night. On entering my compartment, I see, stretched out on the bunk opposite mine, a body that ends in the face of an old woman . . . Am I in the wrong compartment?

I exclaim "Oh! Sorry, ma'am." The face suddenly stares back at me with such incredibly virile hatred that I realize I was mistaken when I thought I was mistaken. "Oh! Sorry, sir." The man does not say another word to me for the entire journey; in the early morning, fully dressed, he turns out to be a kind of manager, some moderately high-ranking civil servant.

EROS

To me, the words "*Il faut*"[27] are erotically charged. This must be because of the reversibility of the two terms: desire and fate. I feel that desire is fate itself, inexorable and implacable; but I also feel that fate is desire: it's the *femme fatale*, Brigitte Helm-Antinea in *L'Atlantide*, whose image was imposed on me forever; when? Was I twelve years old? To me, every woman I am attracted to has the beauty of destiny.

December

RETURN TO CALIFORNIA

Return to San Diego.

I'm glad to come home, not only to Johanne, and not only to the sun, my dives in the ocean, the house; but to this nest of peace, when in Paris I was agitated, restless . . .

I'm glad to pick up the anthropo-socio-biological thread again. Yes, before leaving for Paris, in Paris, and on my return, this new "meditation" has become increasingly essential to me, and it is repressing everything else. I could have taken advantage of the holidays, of having to go to San Francisco and pick up the car Maxime is leaving for me, as an opportunity to immerse myself in hip culture, to pay a visit to all those precious addresses I've written down: Mendecino, Modern Utopia (2441 Le Conte Avenue, Berkeley), the Whole Earth Truck Store (558 Santa Cruz, Menlo Park), etc. But no, I wanted to get back to my reading, and my notes. I've found what really interests me, I think I've begun to understand what I needed to understand about the *nature of society*.

How profoundly resonant I found this passage from Spinoza that Françoise Coblence quoted to me:

"By persistent meditation . . . I came to the conclusion that, *if only I could resolve, wholeheartedly [to change my plan of life]*, I would give up certain evils for a certain good . . . But not without reason did I use these words, 'if only I could resolve in earnest'. For though I perceived these things so clearly in my mind, I still could not, on that account, put aside all greed, desire for sensual pleasure and love of esteem" (*Treatise on the Emendation of the Intellect*[28]).

For the last few days, I haven't been writing down the notes for my new meditation here. In any case, there will be something else apart from this journal, an article or a pamphlet, I'm not sure yet, but whose title will be: *the nature of society* (biology and sociology).

SAN DIEGO

San Diego now has 708,000 inhabitants, overtaking San Francisco

(706,000) to become the second biggest town in California, and the fifteenth biggest in the USA.

The county has 1,366,000 inhabitants; an increase of 60,000, that is, of 4.6% since last July. Of this population 200,000 are Chicanos (15% of the population, but 40% of the unemployed). Twice as many as Blacks (7%, or a little less than 100,000).

CARMEL, BIG SUR

Took the coast road, bringing my new old car from San Francisco back to San Diego, last Friday. (After having Thanksgiving dinner, the night before, with turkey and pumpkin pie, at the Foresters').

Carmel, Big Sur!

The weather was warm, pleasant . . . In Carmel, there's life in the streets, in the main square, with those neo-Mediterraneans, the freaks, the hippies . . . . In Big Sur, the cabins beneath the giant trees . . . I understood the curse of La Jolla, that Californian Monte Carlo, which, instead of being first colonized by the freaks, was colonized by old millionairesses, and retired admirals . . . Perhaps the growing number of students will change things? But the center of vitality is bound to be Del Mar, and not La Jolla.

SURF

They come to surf, hundreds of thousands of them, they come to play with the ocean, and it becomes the most important thing in existence.

SALK INSTITUTE

Back in this astonishing, epic, esoteric, Puritan building . . . But I'm increasingly aware of the void at its center, the beautiful agora; it's a terrace over the ocean, where people can get together, or find themselves again. It's true, when I go for a ten-minute walk around the empty *agora*, I feel a profound unease clouding my profound well-being.

(Problems with it being a meeting place for the researchers; first the basic problem would have to be overcome, which is specialization, the fact that each person is turned in on himself . . . Why not have a mini-forum, every day, open to everybody? . . . No, must think more seriously about this . . .).

On my return, I find that they have installed a dispenser of ass-protectors in all the toilets, circumferences of paper that fit over the seat. This is even more astonishing when you consider that these toilets are almost deserted; they must be used on average once in every twenty-four hours (which doesn't prevent them being cleaned, disinfected, and deodorized several times a day). What's the point of these ass-protectors? Who decided this? Who ordered it to be done? Why?

MARSUPILAMI[29]

I'm getting more and more obsessive; I take my little marsupilamis with me every time I travel. My unconscious is more and more convinced that they protect me. Which means that my unconscious believes that my little girls (they were about thirteen when they gave me this present) are my guardian angels . . .

JONAS AND JOHN

Another conversation with Jonas the prophet (I'm also reading his "writings," and getting a lot out of them); conversations with John.

NEWSPAPERS

The massacre committed last year in a South Vietnamese village by an American army unit.

The occupation of Alcatraz by the Indians.

TWO NEWS ITEMS

One of them shows to what extent the aspiration towards a different kind of life, although repressed by the so-called rational life and by bourgeois civilization, is in fact caused by their aridity. In the United States, this aspiration is ready to spring up at the two weak points in the chain of ages, where adult status begins and ends: it is the adolescents who are responsible for the great rupture, but it is also those who are getting old. Look at Van, the former businessman who became an artisan. Look at the couple who are the subject of the first news item, which I provide a copy of below.

The second news item touches me in a completely different way. It's a tragic destiny, taking its course in the luxury of California, and reaching its miserable conclusion in the opulence of La Jolla. Dorothy Kelly is symbolic of the dark side of Hollywood as well as the dark side of La Jolla. The Hollywood side: she was almost a star, she was beautiful, she expected to be famous, but she missed her chance. The La Jolla side: she was one of those women between two stages in life, stuffed fit to bursting with allowances, revenues, alimony payments, widow's pensions or inheritances, and slowly turning into old painted dolls, with their horrible resistance to aging, their bodies still crazy and their souls even crazier, and at the same time increasingly desiccated by selfishness, pettiness, and futility, wanting to exist and to seduce all the more desperately as solitude closes in around them, and then suddenly precipitated into one of those socio-natural catastrophes which are such a common occurrence here: fire, accident, murder . . .

TELECONNECTION

Phone call from Paris, on Sunday afternoon. From Paris? It's Vincent and Alba, who want me to sign an international petition addressed to General Ovandia, asking him to pardon Régis Debray. The letter is courteous and diplomatic, in the favorable sense of the term. Yes, of course, I'll sign (all the more inclined to help Régis in prison because I want to compensate with a concrete counterweight for the troubled feelings I harbored toward him when he chose the Sartre–Althusser–Fidel path, after I'd pointed out the *Arguments* path to him – although I'm well aware that there *is* no *Arguments* path, that the *Arguments* attitude comes after and not before the *impegno*; that it does not allow a bourgeois background to be exorcised. I know, but I couldn't stop my petty irritation from rising to the surface; it's embarrassing, I'd rather never have started talking about it because whatever happens it'll be embarrassing, either to me or to others, whether I suppress or leave in this passage when I send my manuscript to the publisher). I'm going to try to get Salk's signature, and I suggest that Marcuse should sign. On the phone, Marcuse stops me before I have a chance to read the letter to him: "If Sartre and Monod have signed, that's good enough for me," he says, with all the assurance befitting an intellectual aristocrat. I admire his confidence in circumstances that would arouse my suspicion, as far as petitions are concerned. The next day, I send a telegram to Alba with the signatures on it.

This morning, I called Flo in New York, for the pleasure of speaking to her.

MOLINO ROJO

Goytisolo describes the *Molino Rojo*, in Tijuana. The men sit at tables in front of a long countertop, which serves as a catwalk for the strip-tease girls; they are "bottomless," which means they don't wear panties. Sometimes, as one of these women dances before him, a man will get to his feet, and, spreading his arms like a bird in flight, cover the woman's genitals with his mouth. He saw the grotesque, Goyaesque aspect of the thing, but I sense its sacred, ritual, self-evident aspect.

(A beautiful woman with harmonious features is less sexually appealing than a woman with something misshapen about her, which reproduces in advance, announces, the decomposition of forms in the act of love).

YOUTH

Study:

- Students in the Middle Ages,
- *Sturm und Drang*, the first movement of modern adolescents in

history, already using the same language, eccentric clothes, long hair, as signs of a cultural rupture and symbols of the new culture. Romanticism, they call it today, and they are right, but they pronounce the word with a very stupid disdain (as if they were talking about the most irrelevant and obsolete thing imaginable) for the will to feel, the will to love, the will to live.

(I am sitting at my typewriter in front of a sublime sunset. Oh! I can't describe it. Let's give it a try. In the foreground, the canyon and the hills, dead color. Beyond them lies a bluish-purple strip where the distant ocean and the nebulous sky have mingled together, the horizon no longer tracing its distinctive line. The orange sun, crowned with a strange yellow crest, is plunging into the nebulo-marine strip; I watch its rapid penetration. And then, above, multicolored stripes; the belly of the clouds is here pale orange, there mauve red; their flanks to the East, which is my side, are steel gray. Between the clouds, stretches of sky in palest faded blue. To the East all is gray and cold, to the West all is aflame, ecstatic, in mortal agony).

UTOPIA
Is this a regression to what came before Marx?
Isn't it the rediscovery of everything that was obscured by Marx?

Couldn't neo-naturism and neo-Rousseauism be products of technological development?

Shouldn't socialism advance on two fronts, one macro-political, macro-social, addressing both the problem of the world as a whole and that of each particular society, and the other existential, where experiments are made and the embryos of another kind of life are conceived? But these new nuclei cannot be created *within* the great industrial enterprise (and the revolutionary scope of self-management can only be limited); instead they will emerge outside, to one side (during holidays, in little islands in the course of daily life, among artists and in cultural milieus), beneath (in the neo-craft, neo-archaic sectors), and above it (in the avant-garde sectors of invention and research). It is here that the new foundations will be laid down (oh! There's nothing left but an orange, russet band striping the horizon, caught in the pincers of the night which is rising from the invisible earth and simultaneously descending from the sky). The new existential economy could make partial alliances with capitalism or with the State, and sometimes make use of the State. Its basis must be neo-archaism, including art, on the one hand, and invention on the other: not only scientific or artistic invention, but the invention of new forms of life, of new ways of life. It is invention that will create the new humanity.

COMMUNES

Read an extraordinary text: *Communes, the Contemporary Form of Hip Culture* (mimeograph), by Bob Fitch, a first-hand account by a witness-participant full of critical enthusiasm, as well as synthetic vision.

He locates the problems very clearly. The communes "*are the concentrated manifestation of a culture that wants to survive.*" Having examined the birth, way of life, and organization of several communes, he considers some of their aspects: sex, drugs, economics, books. We learn that sexual liberation may result in a new hierarchy dominated by the "good lovers," that it does not abolish the subservience of women, and that it unleashes a counter-movement towards monogamy. As for drugs, their sacramental and quasi-religious nature (mind-expansion and communion) is well-analyzed.

On the economic level, we see that although the commune in its original or spontaneous form lives parasitically on welfare, unemployment benefit, and family allowances, and has found its own primary resources in rock bands or drug dealing, a growing trend toward autonomy and productivity is beginning to be established.

Bob Fitch tries to define the basic conditions to be met by a commune that wants to survive:

1. an economic basis founded on the sale of products or personal revenue.
2. the acquisition of property or a legal basis sufficient to defend itself against the local authorities (the police are making increasing numbers of raids, which dislocate the communes);
3. the regular payment of bills;
4. *playing it cool with drugs*: being careful about using drugs in front of outsiders, and taking the necessary precautions in anticipation of raids;
5. the presence of adults who have had experience of hip life in its entirety;
6. a period of friendship or initiation prior to setting up the commune;
7. an attempt to establish positive links with the neighboring community;
8. the predominance of what can be created over what can be experienced (it's clear that in the case of spontaneous or primitive communes, what mattered was not survival, but to have good experiences. "Whether the commune lasted for three days or three years, if people said at the end of it that 'a good thing happened', that was enough in itself").

And Bob Fitch considers the *hip commune* to be a *frontier life-style.* Like all historical frontiers, *"the community is comprised of drop-outs and push-outs, and put-outs. Only here we are experiencing outs who create their culture within the society."*

(Yes, the new frontier is not only defined by developments in technology and science: it's here as well . . . .).

By way of conclusion, the author describes himself: "I'm twenty-nine years old, I'm a minister of the United Church of Christ, married, with one child. It's a long family tradition: my father, my grandfather and my great grandfather, a clergyman, went before me. It has always been part of our family tradition to keep one foot in this society and one foot on the frontier. It's probably for this reason that we have always loved frontier people. I find hip minds curious and active. I believe that the things they have chosen to devote themselves to, drugs, sex, new life styles, the significance and the meaninglessness of work, the use of the rural or urban terrain, are a prophecy of a time to come . . . "

We visited the *San Diego Free Press* commune, for a party to celebrate its new activities (the transformation of the bimonthly paper, which is becoming a weekly, and is changing its format; the opening of the coffee shop). As we arrived, the police were leaving. Plainclothes police officers had gone in unannounced, and had arrested the bartenders, on the pretext that they were distributing liquor without a license. A policeman had gone into a girl's bedroom, where he found some pill she'd been given without a prescription. They arrested the girl, Ian and another guy, and didn't let them go until the early hours. They didn't dare cart off the volunteer bartenders from outside the commune, like Mang, who was only cautioned. We stayed behind to discuss what had happened. I met a very nice pastor who runs the New Adult group (which I must explore, too). Some of the commune members and their friends, who are often bearded, wear badges in their buttonholes, big portraits of Mao on a red background, which give me some bad vibrations. Another wears a black badge reading "anarchy." They show two films, one on the Black Panthers: militias are forming, training, doing maneuvers; their leaders make incomprehensible declarations (the sound is very poor); then it's Joris Ivens' film on Vietnam, a mixture of documentary truth and brainwash, which I find extremely disturbing.

The arrest yesterday of the presumed murderers of Sharon Tate, hippies and commune-dwellers, is going to aggravate the reprobation and repression . . .

John thinks I could get money from a foundation to do a study on the communes. At once, this idea slackens my tension even more; it had already begun to weaken when I began my ovulation on the "nature of society." I want to put off my desire to immerse myself in the communes until some time in the future. (Must draw up the research project).

I need to think some more about my profound and irresistible passion for the commune problem, despite the fact that I personally have already found the lifestyle that suits me, and I'm fighting to hold on to it, and deepen it, rather than change it. I can't see myself living in a commune. On the contrary, I want to protect my marginality, my solitary craftsmanship. I want to hold on to my status as a CNRS researcher, which provided me and continues to provide me with a regular income for my irregular, free, self-determined work . . . But I still feel a strong personal concern for the communes, because the energy and the priority they devote to love, friendship, the search for one's own truth, fraternity, and reconciliation, all fortify what I think is truest in myself; I gather my pollen, I make my honey . . . Yes, this cultural revolution, like May 1968, brings me more closely in touch with myself, with my truths. It confirms me and encourages me in my resistance to techno-bureaucracy, bourgeois life, things that aren't important . . .

And what's more, these communes represent the reviving avatar of communism, which I cannot resolve to forget, to abandon. I know, I know, I want to know, I want to know its dead-ends, its failures, its shortcomings . . . For I am not seeking the magic formula, the historical solution; what I seek is the rebirth of hope, or rather it's hope in its nascent state, the rising sap of hope: it's the overwhelming joy I get from everything that sets out to shatter loneliness, everything that sets out for love.

Oh yes . . .

(And night has fallen; for a long time now I have been alone in the Salk Institute; in my window all I can see is the reflection of my office, with the posters that I stuck on the wall, the map of America, the face of a Hawaiian girl that I stole from a United Airlines brochure, a booted beauty in a miniskirt from I forget which advertisement . . . Right, that's it, I'm going home, my beautiful, good Johanne is waiting for me).

(Try to analyze these young people's hatred of private property, their need for both impoverishment and community).

Sunday, 7 December

THE ECOLOGY MOVEMENT

The pollution alert springs in part from the cultural revolution, and in part from the mainstream evolution of American society. Two kernels of anti-pollutionist awareness have formed, one at institutional level (the political, economic, technological, and academic establishments). And at this level, a process has been set in motion, in the American way, which means that there has been a delay in the detection of the danger itself and, that initially, intervention has been dissipated, disorganized, and slow to get off the ground.

The *polis* has now been warned about smog pollution in the atmosphere, caused by toxic fumes from factories, and car and airplane engines, and about the pollution and destruction of plant and animal environments (not only has DDT been found in the ocean's anchovies, but also lead from the gases burned by engines and refineries). The government is considering technical solutions to preserve the national heritage, as well as prohibitions which could one day go as far as banning the combustion engine, and which will speed up the widespread adoption of "clean" atomic energy, etc.

The University is also tackling this problem, not only through research into different kinds of pollution, but also through the emergence and creation of a new discipline, ecology, the science of Man's relationship with his environment. But what's really striking is the way in which the war on pollution and the ecological apostolate have been taken up by the cultural revolution. The "eco-groups" which have formed among students and young people are one of the efflorescences, one of the pseudopodia, of this extraordinarily diverse movement, which is also the anti-war, anti-ghetto, anti-establishment movement, and is now seeking Reconciliation with Nature. The New Left (with the article in the September or October issue of *Ramparts* which I mentioned about the death of the ocean) and the young activists from the "eco-groups" have played an absolutely decisive role in the development of the new obsession with pollution, which has been pouring out for the past few months, with no sign of stopping, in the magazines and newspapers (last Sunday there were long articles in the *West* supplement of the *Los Angeles Times*, and in the *San Diego Union*). So it's the eco-activists who are making society aware of the sickness that is threatening to destroy it. They're acting as a warning system. But while the *polis* is seeking technical solutions, the eco-movement is calling the validity of the *polis* itself into question, and its identification of the main problem is radical: above and beyond the problem of the social system, there is the problem of life *in* and *of* the planet Earth, the life of Man. And here we are, caught up in the dialectic of history: will the revolutionary eco-movement serve chiefly as a stimulant to social conservatism, or will its biological conservatism take on a revolutionary social significance? For the first time, and concerning a problem other than the Vietnam war, the cultural revolution now has the opportunity to get its message heard at every level of public opinion, and to act in a more broad-based manner, as well as in depth. I believe that the eco-movement marks the New Left's entry into anthropolitics.

The eco-movement constitutes a genuine point of convergence between the neo-Rousseauism of hip culture and the Marxist vulgate of the New Left. One aspect of this is represented by Clifford Humphrey, the 32-year-old founder of Ecology Action in Berkeley. A former highway construction engineer, he wrecked his family car, a 1958 Rambler, made a sculpture out of it, and has been getting around by bicycle, on foot or hitch-hiking ever since. The other aspect, represented by the same Clifford Humphrey, is a denunciation of capitalism, which he holds responsible for pollution: "When you're only interested in maximum profit, the result is maximum pollution."[30] But he goes beyond both the hippie vulgate and the Marxist vulgate, when he follows up his denunciation of capitalism by calling economic growth itself into question, in the name of the well-being of humanity, and because the alternative he proposes is not just a form of socialism devoted to the good functioning of society, but also a system "which would take the best possible care of the Earth." Here we see the reemergence, in its nascent state, of a religion of Life, of Nature, and of the Earth, which implies an extraordinary reversal in the relationship between Man and nature. Man should no longer be the master, sovereign and possessor of nature. It is nature that must make its revolution within Man: "the highest level of revolutionary awareness must be found in the classes that have been most ruthlessly exploited: animals, trees, water, air . . . . " is Gary Snyder's extraordinary formulation.

So "green power" is born! Gary Snyder expresses, with great lucidity, the notion that the green revolution must be waged, not against Man, but within Man, and this dialectic reveals the orientation of the new humanism: "Man has reached the point where he must become smaller in order to grow."

Another key phrase from the new humanism: "*We have met the enemy at last, and it was us.*" (Cliff Humphrey doubts that ecological deterioration and damage can be avoided; he fears that it's too late, but he forces himself to be optimistic: "*Pessimism has no survival value*").

SCHEMA OF THE CULTURAL REVOLUTION

NATURE . . . . MAN				
Experience of a new way of life (hippies)	The new family (communes)	The new relationship with the world (eco-action)	The new society (more community, more individuality)	The new politics (not yet formulated[31])

THE MY LAI MASSASCRE

"The price of eternal vigilance is indifference."
McLuhan

The massacre took place a year and a half ago, in March 1968: although the news of it was immediately obstructed, smothered (an inquiry by the US army at the time buried the affair), it was not entirely destroyed, and so with time, with the disbanding of those charged with the repression, general and personal demoralization, the obsessive working of remorse in some, and an institutional and puritanical sense of justice in others, the news emerged and was reported. And now it has been broadcast everywhere; every TV station, every newspaper, even reactionary ones like the *San Diego Union*, and all the big magazines, are describing the massacre, and meditating on it . . .

Astonishingly, the American conscience is unperturbed by the anonymous, statistical massacre perpetrated by the massive air and artillery bombardments: because, as they see it, "that's how war is," forgetting that this war hits civilians harder than soldiers; what horrifies America is the atrocity that one person perpetrates against another, it's the deliberate murder of women and children that *you can see. You know that you are killing because you can see that you are killing.* This is the point at which you feel yourself to be a murderer, and therefore guilty.

Naturally, in the self-questioning around the My Lai affair, all the processes offering escape from responsibility have been set in motion; we are reminded that the Vietcong also practice revenge and extermination – and *they* do it systematically, add the reporters; we are reminded of the Oradour and the Babi Yar Massacres perpetrated by the Nazis, the Stalinist exterminations, and the Algerian civilians killed by the French during the Algerian War: but we also observe the emergence, in *Time* magazine, of a sort of proud humility, which refuses to excuse America by relegating her to the common lot of nations at war. What counts as acceptable behavior for the French, Germans or Russians sullies America's desired self-image. "For *them* it's only to be expected, but for *us*, it's unthinkable."

What struck me on reading this issue of *Time*, which was almost entirely devoted to the massacre, was the force and the insistence of this self-questioning, and examination of conscience, which are currently unimaginable in most other countries, either because they are prohibited by censorship, or because the press itself helps to censor the problem, which was the case in France during the Algerian war. *Time* casts light on exactly what ought to be seen as scandalous, namely:

a) The latent racism that underlies this collective massacre and makes it possible (the Vietnamese are "gooks," just as the Algerians were "coons" to the French).

b) The fact that the killers, like the lieutenant who commanded them, were ordinary, average men.

So, although the massacre can be explained in part by the circumstances, and can be considered, even if it is not an isolated event, to be one of those inevitable "errors" which happen in anti-guerilla warfare, *Time* avoids attributing the evil to an exceptional circumstance or to an atypical or deviant group: many of the killers were drafted recruits, they were ordinary citizens, raised on the sacred principles of religion, morality, and the American Constitution . . .

And once again I'm confronted with the paradox of America: it is certainly the most barbaric of the civilized countries, but it is also the most civilized of the barbaric countries (and all countries are barbaric).

There's an interesting short study to be made of the process through which the information concerning this affair came to light. 1st phase: obstruction and smothering of information; 2nd phase: the information goes underground, lies dormant; 3rd phase: a (young) veteran writes to the Congress, the Senate and the Secretary of State, reactivating the information; 4th phase: a few members of the House take this letter into consideration; 5th phase: its first emergence in a minor press agency; 6th phase: general broadcast. Also look into the question of photos: a photographer was present at the massacre, and he shot as much film as he could, immediately before and immediately after the people were executed. And the most striking photo is of a group of women and children, showing an old woman whose face is frozen in a grimace of terror, another woman hiding behind her with her arms around her, and a third woman, a young mother with her baby, who seems distracted by something, or busy scratching the skin on her belly. (All in color, and blown up, in *Life* magazine).

THE UNKNOWN

Reading (in a fairly interesting and curious article in the *Los Angeles Free Press*, "Techno-anarchy"), this sentence: "The observatory is humanity's most highly symbolic structure: a temple to the unknown," I began to think: the unknown, the unknown, it's not some sector, domain, or zone of shadow which simply surrounds the known; no, it's the principle, the subject (if there is a subject in this shady affair), it is what animates all things and what animates us . . .

SOLIDARITIES

The *Open Door Society* of San Diego, a society for trans-racial adoption. It's an association founded by a dozen families who have adopted children of all races, black and brown (Mexicans, Indians), and who work outside the adoption agencies, wanting to encourage people to "love children and to find a home for all children." I must go and see these trans-racial families as well. (PO Box 2447, San Diego Calif 92112, tel. 239 3179).

NEW *EMILE*

On tolerance: if a mouse from family A receives a suspension of cells from a mouse from family B while in the womb, it will accept a transplant from family B after it is born. But if it has received nothing before it is born, it will reject the B transplant.

The intrauterine stage is the stage of induced immunological tolerance. As far as ideas are concerned, the stage of induced immunological tolerance can only be that of our earliest education, in the family and at school; we must therefore learn how to inject B ideas (the universal ideas, which are incessantly destroyed or reduced by psychic allergies to other people) during this first era of childhood.

It is understandable that tolerance is most often found in cultural mongrels like ourselves; in any case we are of all people the most inclined to tolerate, and so it is up to us to train and educate a multi-racial humanity, *in which one does not reject the other's heart.*

Initiation: the anthropo-sociological equivalent of a vaccination?

Let the individual overcome his crises on his own, form his own defenses, his own immunology.

Nobility and wisdom, the primary goals of education; perceptiveness and intelligence, secondary goals. (Don't put it like that, correct all of this).

ASTONISHMENT

It's so incredible! The mouth is used for speaking, eating, and breathing (and yet we don't have three mouths); the penis is used for pissing and ejaculating!

One mouth and not two.

Two eyes and not one.

Two nostrils and one nose.

How different it might all have been!

THE HONEY MOON

At this seminar, I find out why the moon on the horizon looks bigger to our eyes than when it's at its zenith. It is not because atmospheric phenomena deform our vision; no, it is because our mind conceives of the sky as being a slightly flattened hemispherical vault. The horizon always looks further away to us than the zenith. What's more, our minds reduce our vision of objects to a standard average size, which is that of perceptual consistency . . . In fact, our eyes see the moon as being the same size at its zenith and at the horizon, but to our minds, seeing the same size further away means that the moon must be bigger.

MYSTERY

All the world's mystery is in our minds.
All of our minds' structures are projected outward, onto the world.
The heart (but not the key?) of the mystery is within us . . .

EAST–WEST

Why are these defenders of freedom so vigilant in the West and so negligent in the East? Why don't we concern ourselves with the prisons in the East as we concern ourselves with those in the West? What's the point of asking the question? I know why. Woe betide us.

EXPERIENCE

Between amnesia and bitterness lies experience.

UNDERSTANDING

We might be capable of understanding everything very soon, apart from the things that really matter. Why?

ADVANCING

Advancing on one front means either advancing or retreating on another front, in any case transforming the other fronts.

JONAS SALK (QUOTATIONS)

"The bionauts," a magnificent expression: man is a navigator in Life, a navigator through Life (compare this with my "Spaceship Earth").

"The solutions of the past have become the inhibitors of the future" (*Man's View of Himself*, Canadian Public Health Assn., Toronto, 1962).

"The orthodoxies of the present are made with the revolutions of the past" (*ibid.*, p. 4).

"When the method has been found, the stuff of dreams becomes the stuff of existence" (*Man, the Trustee of Evolution*, Washington D.C., June 1962).

DIALECTICS

The dialectical principle is at work in every being. It is the permanent antagonism of contrary needs, and in fact constitutes the organizing principle of life. It is the fundamental duality, which is active from the roots of our being to the manifestations of our personality. It is the permanent presence of contradictory virtualities, which are aroused in all circumstances to confront every event. And this, paradoxically, is what explains the predominance of non-dialectical thought: since action is a choice between alternatives, the lazy mind tends to imitate behavior, and favors alternative thinking, excluding what is contrary, and refusing to admit contradiction.

Clearly, it is because contradiction is always present that it always has to be banished, and it is because it is always present that it always poses the alternative (Have I expressed myself correctly?)

Berque: "A menacing negativity accompanies human progress."

Trend and counter-trend: the counter-trend can be: 1. integrated, 2. contrary, 3. disintegrative.

Every principle is ambivalent, contradictory, depending on the interplay of forces. Study the interplay of forces as closely as possible.

The truth is, this is a time when several societal structures are possible.

UTOPIANISM

Utopianism is both what changes reality and what is incapable of changing it. Realism is both lucid and blind.

DIALECTICAL WISDOM

Dialectics tells us to be wary of words. It teaches us to see positivity and negativity, duality and impotence, in every concept. It is the art of thinking that plays with words, and makes some of its most brilliant discoveries in plays on words . . .

CLINICAL SOCIOLOGY

"Clinical sense often anticipates clinical science" (J. Salk, *The Humanities from the View Point of a Biologist*, University of Minnesota, November 1961, p. 19).

SOCIAL DEMOCRACY

The socialist parties foster the hope of great change. When they get into power, nothing happens. Then they pretend to be astonished by the reactions of those who had believed in change: "Come now, you're not being realistic!"

INVENTION

"Very often, the most important discoveries are made by individuals who do not belong to the specialized field that they have renewed, or who did not know that, according to official opinion, the discovery that they have just made was impossible" (S. Moscovici, "Le Marxisme et la question naturelle," *L'Homme et la Société*, 13, p. 103).

DECOLONIZATION

It is nations and peoples that attain freedom, and not individuals. Once the emancipated nation has achieved freedom of action, and is engaged in the struggle for survival or development, it continues or increases the oppression of individuals. (The profound ambiguity of freedom; national liberation and civil liberties).

Thursday, 11 December

THE MASSACRE

Discussion the day before yesterday, at our house, which reminded me of discussions at the end of the Algerian War. While they were all talking, expressing their vehemence or distress, I was also thinking about something else: that whether the consequences are minor or far-reaching, and whether or not public opinion has been moved by this affair, what seems positive to me is that the truth has been told, revealed, and made public. It's the fact that it managed to emerge after a year and a half of smothering and asphyxia. The Stalinist experience gave me a virulent allergy to the stifling of information, and I still have it.

RADIO

In the morning, when we wake up, in the evening, before we go to sleep, the beauty of these voices, these songs . . . *Yesterday*, *Rain*.

AND IT WORKS

Two rational systems, two wasteful systems; in the capitalist system, there is rationality in the permanent stimulant provided by competition, or at least by the market, in the Darwinian effect of natural selection, but there is also waste in this same competition, in the system of profit, in the cancerous proliferation of the economics of futility; as for so-called socialism, its rationality lies in central planning, and its conscientious care for the economy, but its wastefulness lies in its bureaucracy. Which has been the most wasteful up to now? The Stalinist or Stalinistic system, with its wholesale destruction of intelligence, material, and men, with its stifling of economic creativity beneath bureaucratic-dogmatic sclerosis, or the USA, where the economy has been abandoned to an anarchic deluge of profit and desire? (Couldn't this question be considered statistically?)

THE MURDER OF THE PANTHERS

And while America is asking itself painful questions about the massacre in a Vietnamese village, Black Panthers are being killed; today, in Los Angeles, yesterday in Chicago. The police are making raids, and the battle has begun. In fact, all of the leaders have now been killed, imprisoned, or exiled. Here, on the radio, in the papers, these are small, isolated news items. In reality, it's an attempt at the federal level to destroy the Black nation before it can be born.

THE MURDERERS OF SHARON TATE

I find these faces fascinating. This murder is a rite.

NIXON

Nixon on TV. For me, there's always a dissociation between faces and ideas; I am incapable of seeing the faces of my political enemies as contemptible.

Monday, 15 December

THE GOSPEL ACCORDING TO SAINT MOLECULE

Finished the fourth volume of J. Salk's writings. Reading this has gorged me with vitamins.

My notes are accumulating, masses of them, and their center of gravity is bio-sociology. I've at last discovered the massive hiatus in my anthropocosmology (*Vif du sujet*). The missing link, or rather the keystone, is biotics!

What an extraordinary, decisive moment this is for me. Here I am at the center of gravity, at the center of my intellectual gravitations.

And there's something else: a fantastic messianic enthusiasm, encouraged by the presence of Jonas and perhaps also by Californian mysticism (yes, there's something in the air here). Jonas: the gospel according to Saint Molecule.

And I'm writing (typing) this, in this blessed place, in front of my window at the Salk, just as the sun, facing me, is turning red. The looping jets from the air base have traced two hieroglyphic signs in the sky. Every day, every day, at the same time, there's this celebration in the west . . . Yesterday, as soon as the sun went down, a crescent moon took its place.

My systematic reading has come to an end, for the time being. I'm going to put my notes in order, try to structure a plan, and then off I go. I'm very impatient to start writing up.

Yesterday, I watched the sun as it sank to the horizon, then covered my eyes with my palms. I saw the sun at the end of the tunnel, at the bottom of the pit, of the abyss within myself.

Then I watched it fall into the sea: I was trying to catch a glimpse of the green ray.

HOW CAN THE FOLLOWING BE RECONCILED?

1. The self is a myth.
2. Find yourself.

BORIS DE SCHLOEZER

News of Boris de Schloezer's death reaches me two months late, through the article Gaëtan Picon devoted to him in *Le Monde*. A gentle, elegant hand taps on the wall of indifference. For a while I remain on the other side of the wall, surprised by this presence, the living irruption of a man I had not seen for so long.

Time and distance are a greater death than death itself. And death itself suddenly comes close for an instant, the last spark before forgetting . . .

MARCUSE

Jonas, the Mangs, the MacAllisters, Chantal and the Marcuses came to dinner. When the conversation turns to politics, I feel estranged from their view of things. Of the Black Panthers, who are resisting police raids by opening fire on them, Marcuse says: "That's their business . . . Nothing to do with us." I feel as far removed from this fear of criticizing as I do from the American liberals' naïve criticism: "They shouldn't do that."

M. detests America; or no, that's not right, instead he's established a metabolic relationship with America that allows him to vent his bile and his adrenaline, and means that while he's busy detesting and despising, he is also very pleased, very much at ease.

I ask him privately why he doesn't go and live in France. He tells me that the situation there is dreadful, that repression is getting worse. He has just met André G. in New York: "He told me the police intercept his mail every morning, open it, read it, and then give it back to the concierge."

Me (to myself): ?! . . .

His wife announces delightedly that Sartre has declared his complete and wholehearted adherence to Marxism, in the latest issue of the *New Left Review*. She scrutinizes my face to savor the rapture that these glad tidings ought to arouse in me. I try to look pleased. I can't manage it, so I say:

"I thought that had already happened a few years ago."

"This time, it's for real."

Me (finally managing to look delighted): "Aha!"

MARXISM

Marxism: the less it explains, the more convincing it is.

How anti-scientific Marxism is, in its arrogance and its intimidation!

The dogmatic-religious nature of Marxism is revealed precisely by its arrogance and its intimidation of any attempt at revision, always judged to be objectively and subjectively disastrous, pernicious, degraded, and degrading. Indeed this intolerance, this allergy (the rejection of every foreign or new element) is characteristic of the creature that is Marxism.

SCIENTIFIC THEORY AND UNSCIENTIFIC THEORY

Their content may be exactly the same. But unscientific theory immunologically rejects any foreign element and tries to avoid modification at any price.

MANICHAEISM

What disturbs me most in their Manichaeism is not that they paint an exaggeratedly sombre picture of the West, but that they whiten the East.

WORRY

At ten in the evening, we listened to the commentator's diatribe on Channel 5. He holds Marcuse responsible for manufacturing the drug that is perverting young brains, and of calling in his book, another *Mein Kampf* (*Towards the Liberation*), for the violent destruction of American society. Marcuse bursts out laughing. For my part, I see it as a call to murder. In other circumstances, I say to myself . . . But perhaps these circumstances are already in place? The next morning, as I'm backing the Rambler out of the garage, I see a man at the wheel of one of the cars that are parked in the street, holding a piece of paper in his hand and apparently looking at me. Immediately, I think he's a spy, perhaps from some secret police agency, come to keep watch over the house where Marcuse dined the night before. I pretend not to have seen him, watching him all the while out of the corner of my eye as I make my maneuvers (and the fact that apparently he doesn't notice me seems just as worrying a sign as if he had stared me straight in the face). I arrive at the Salk, and say nothing to Johanne on the phone about my apprehension. When I come home at midday, the car's still there, but the driver has gone. Nonchalantly, I stroll over to inspect it, and inside I see some oceanographic documents. So he was just a researcher from the Scripps, and not a cop or an assassin.

THE MASSACRE

They – people who belong to the "New Left" – concentrate on one aspect of the affair: the enormous publicity given to the My Lai massacre has provoked no strong emotion; and worse still, it's being treated as one news item among others, it's even making people feel good about themselves: "Look how righteous we are." Well, yes, all right, but that's not the whole story, and, to my mind, this truth is grafted onto another truth, of another kind, namely the emergence of the truth.

POLITICS

We still know almost nothing about politics. This is not only because we are implicated in it, and ill informed about it, but also because it's so extraordinarily difficult to understand.

THE EVENT

Everybody assimilates the event in their own way, which means that they change its properties, and destroy it, all the while believing that they are giving it its true meaning.

MR. SPOCK

He's my favorite character. At 5.45, I rush to turn on the TV for the latest episode of *Star Trek*.

IN PASSING

The other night, heard Jonas saying "Fatality and futility." With reference to what?

DINNER

Dinner tonight at the Orgels' place; don't forget to ask him about my hypothesis, which may be idiotic, concerning the origin of life.

THE FREE PRESS COMMUNE

Someone threw a stone through the window of the commune's house, and the landlord has decided to evict his tenants. Yesterday, on TV, I saw the commune's family bus heading a demonstration by young marines against the Vietnam war.

THE TATE AFFAIR

The wandering gang, the horde, the mystical family led by Manson-Jesus. Here there is truly a rupture, a tear in the social fabric, which allows us to contemplate the abyss. For this is the abyss of our own society, of our own culture, and furthermore it directly communicates with the great anthropological pit of Padirac.[32]

POLLUTION

Isn't the sense of *internal* pollution essential here? All the drinks which, only a month ago, proudly announced that they contained cyclamates, are now labeled in big letters: Cyclamate-free, sugar added; the alternative is sugar, precisely what the cyclamates were supposed to substitute . . .

CIVILIZATION

Civilization must be at once preserved and transformed. Perhaps this contradiction is insurmountable.

11%

The percentage of murders has risen by 11% in the first nine months of 1969, compared with last year.

ADULT

In the *Nouvel Observateur*, an interview with Durand Dassier, who lived at Day-Top, a self-detoxification center for addicts. Suddenly, I find this formulation illuminating: "Being an adult means being capable of having a relationship with yourself when alone; it also means being able to reach out and love others, taking the risk that they may reject you." (And of course, he admits that there are no real adults, that all of us are more or less infantile).

Then the following, which is much more dubious, because it's unequivocal: "It is freedom that creates anxiety, and not rules." Anxiety is caused by rules as well as freedom, and although rules are doubtless a response to the anxiety of being free, freedom is also a response to the anxiety of having rules.

SUB-BOURGEOISIE

An important notion, to be sure, which I find in D. Desanti's article on Los Angeles and the Angela Davis affair (in *Le Monde*, which I read this morning in the library). When segments of ethnic groups that are subjugated or judged to be inferior rise to bourgeois standards, they are rejected or, at least, not integrated into the dominant (White) bourgeoisie, and psychologically they are sent back to the ghetto of their ethnic group. Hence the growth of revolutionary nationalism.

(Link this to the question of the intelligentsia in relation to the national problem).

RADAR

There are so many interesting things to read . . . , you just can't do it . . . you can only read by radar.

MARGINAL PEOPLE

"A strange bond often exists among anti-social types in their capacity to see environments as they really are." (McLuhan, *The Medium is the Message*).

Wednesday, 21 December

(Have begun, with difficulty, writing up a socio-biological introduction).

CHEMISTRY OF IDEAS

Bio-chemistry of ideas: how values of consolation or compensation become values for anti-establishment activity. The problem of the renewed virulence of Christian values (fraternity, salvation), which are detaching themselves from the mass of official values, and are beginning to play an antagonistic role; all this keeps going round in my head. I'd like to do some thinking about the biochemistry of ideas, their conditions of association and dissociation, etc. (Memo to myself).

THOUGHT

Thought is what every individual, and every secret group, produces in the intellectual order to justify and defend itself. Thought is a weapon and a form of semantic armor. But thought is also what will pierce this armor one day, or rather emerge from it, to go forth naked, searching.

CYBERNETIC POEM

In the book on cybernetic art works that I consulted at Crichton's, I came across a poem, which I think was composed by SAM (Stochastic Analogous Machine), the computer, and whose title, which I think is *Stafford Beer*, seems to me full of poetic humor. I read, marveling:

"What lies between rigidity and chaos.
Which both have their art and their science? . . . "

and:

"Will the next toss yield heads or tails?"

and:

"Random events conspire toward a particular pattern."

Monday, 28 December

MAO

Having noted this sentence from Mao: "It is always the people with the least knowledge who overturn those who have the most," I started thinking about this man Mao; unlike Stalin, he loves to meditate about the world. A wise man; he may be bigoted, but he's also cosmic.

WRITING UP

I'm trying to structure my plan, and therefore my whole paper. I? . . . It is thought, the organizing power, that is trying to make its combinations, its associations, and do its assembling through me . . . It is expectant, feeling its way, impatient. I would be convinced that it won't succeed in conferring an order and a structure on all these molecules of disparate ideas, which I've been accumulating haphazardly for the past three months, if I didn't remember the same distress, the same doubts, every time I have set to work . . . And again I'm experiencing, suffering, the same nausea, disgust, headaches, this drama of childbirth from which a work will emerge whose author I will pretend to be.

Yes, (for me) thought is what begins with the juxtaposition of raw material, of isolated ideas, and attempts to link them together into a form.

BIRDS

On the seashore, in Mission Bay, we stand on the veranda of this California style fisherman's café (fishing as a sport and not a job) and throw crumbs to the seagulls, pigeons and sparrows that gather about us; the sparrows are the most daring, and come the nearest, the pigeons more cautious, but less fearful than in France; the timid, suspicious seagulls keep two or three yards away. Every man for himself! Each does its best to steal food from its neighbor or congener.

This determined individual egotism is also as far as possible from being individual; it is imposed by natural selection, allowing the most vigorous and the strongest to triumph. It is genetically predetermined by the species, for the survival of the species.

Each struggles against its congeners, and therefore against its own species, but at the same time, for its own species. This fact reveals, among other things, the universal ambivalence of all of life.

INDIANS

Photos of archaic Indians in the Museum of Man in San Diego. The most primitive of them from the technical point of view, the ones that go almost naked are, like the Amazonian Indians or the extinct Alakalufs of Tierra del Fuego, those with the most beautiful faces in the world. A feeling of irreparable tragedy.

Went looking for the Indians in the reservations around San Diego. There are ten reservations indicated on the map, in territories outside the system of roads, with no towns marked in them. Searched in vain for the Syacuan Indians, down a canyon path, between arid mountains. On our way back, a young hitchhiker we picked up told us that there are fifteen of them left, up there in the mountains.

FACES

Jotted this down at San Diego airport, where I was an hour early, waiting for the plane carrying the girls and the Burgs. I was looking at the faces around me in a state close to fascination. The comet-like faces of airports, passing by so quickly, going elsewhere, carrying off their mystery with them. Most of the women's faces are hideous, dry and empty masks, but the faces of elderly women are truly moving, and more so than elsewhere. Some of these faces strike you like lightning . . .

Such different faces and yet such a uniform civilization. Nearly all of them have something uncouth about them.

The crowd is plebeian, and yet bourgeois wealth is greater here than elsewhere. These plebeian faces have not managed to become bourgeois as quickly as their lifestyles, their cars, their refrigerators, their home furnishings, etc.

INTERNAL POLLUTION

DDT, and even aspirin, de-stabilizes our organism's biochemical equilibrium, Martin Weigett tells me.

Apparently, fat stores harmful waste products; going on a diet is enough to send a sudden flood of them into the liver.

STEREO

At Crichton's: he puts these amazing, enormous, padded stereophonic speakers over my ears. And it's not just a torrent of music that surges in through my ears, but a rippling galaxy of harmonies, entering my head, flooding the whole inside of my body, all the way down to my feet. I'm possessed! And that *Rolling Stones* record . . .

BAYOU COUNTRY

Everything on this Credence Clearwater Revival LP transports me. Especially *The Graveyard Train.*

STATISTICS

California, the most highly populated state in the Union, numbered 20 million inhabitants on Christmas night.

8 million marijuana users in the United States. 180,000 heroin users.

FUTUROLOGY

The future is not built on foresight, but on the capacity for change (I don't know where I stole this idea from).

USA

The young are either saving or killing off American society. Or rather, they are saving it and killing it at the same time.

THE HEART

"Only do what makes your heart leap" (Alan Gregg).

SOCIALISM

Think about this sentence from Jacques Viard, the author of a thesis on Péguy. "Péguy defended only one cause: socialism, which is to say the hope for a city uniting the minimum social pressure with the maximum social communication."

FAMILY

Irène and Véro are here for ten days, with Evelyne and Andrée. Françoise, who stayed for a week, has left.

Yesterday I was happy, playing the patriarch, driving my family in the eight-seater station wagon through mountains and desert.

January–February 1970

I've decanted myself. I've started diverting everything to do with the *Nature of Society* away from this journal. Already the embryo of something bigger than an article – a book – has begun to live inside me. I'm also collecting my *Notes on Life* elsewhere, because they're no longer isolated sketches; they've become a sort of experimental exploration, which is now also autonomous.

And so here I am, immersed in the *Notes on Life* and in the *Nature of Society*. I'm closing the doors around me. San Francisco, music, and movies have all faded into the background. My first foray into the "cultural revolution" is over. I feel that I'm bursting with pollen that I haven't yet assimilated, or transformed. I'm counting on the study which I've put off until later for a chance to delve deeper.

I'm working. In this month of January, have I achieved serenity at last? I feel so good to be working: cultivating my mind, thinking. What peace, what joy. Peace and joy have grown, blossomed during these tribal weeks, with family and friendship intermingled, and everything I feel is so personal, so intimate, so coenesthesic that I don't know how to translate and express it in this journal. And so the lifeblood of this journal is flowing elsewhere, into my work, into my life, and only a few drops run in here from time to time.

PEOPLE'S COMMUNE

The *San Diego Free Press* commune (which calls itself the *People's Commune*) has been attacked several times: there have been raids by persons unknown on the writing center and the printing press (destroyed), and death threats. The heroic little paper is continuing to provoke and defy military power (propaganda aimed at the marines bound for Vietnam), police power (denunciation of the raids on the Black Panthers), the power of capital (this miniscule David lampoons the *San Diego Union*'s Goliath). I have the feeling they are going to be crushed.

LIGHTS

Lights slip along the waterfront in the night. These lights are cars. Inside these cars, these incredibly complex machines, are men, souls, consciousnesses. *We know that.* What do we know of the other lights that burn in the sky?

ROGERS[33]

He's an idiot! He's washed up! Every attempt I make to meet Carl Rogers fails in the face of his indifference, and I don't push it too much. But in the end, stimulated by the presence of the piquant Escoffier-Lambiotte woman, I convince myself that it's absolutely essential she should meet him, so that I can meet him. I'm warned before the meeting that there's been a schism in his "Center for Studies of the Person," and that he's almost alone there now. A well-proportioned villa, on the great high hill, and a man with a handsome mask of a face, but bitter, incapable of tearing himself away from his fixed idea.

All this is true, *however* his fixed idea is also the vital idea that he has given us: it's a simplistic, childish, basic idea; but in this it resembles all great isolated and hypostasized truths. It isn't yet the new *Emile*, but it is the necessary anti-*Emile*: "*Learning is great. Teaching is ridiculous.*" (Read *Freedom to Learn*, Merrill, 1969).

DISNEYLAND

Another visit to Disneyland, on our return from Los Angeles. Disneyland is grotesque, and it shows, reveals the nature of modern tourism, in and by virtue of its grotesqueness.

WHALES

They pass by, on their way from the Arctic Ocean to the warm waters of Baja California, where they gather and mate. They travel in little groups, playing, flirting, cavorting about, enormous and agile in the water. Sometimes you can see a brief white shimmer, or a powerful jet of water . . . It's the beginning of the world. It's Bernardin de Saint-Pierre . . . I can't explain why these playful whales make me so happy.

AMERICA

D. comes from an orthodox Brooklyn Jewish family, and has always lived in New York, the most cosmopolitan city in the world. At the age of twenty-four, he had never met a single goy.

Phoned Stanley. I tell him that I may come back via India and ask him for some addresses. He talks about New York. The number of neighborhoods which are dangerous at night is growing, there are more and more muggings; in the last few days there have been three or four attacks in his building. "It's as if the city was disintegrating before my eyes," he says.

We see the young multi-millionaire on TV, giving away his riches like a hippie Santa Claus. He's convinced that he has found the solution to the Vietnam war: he's going to camp out in front of the White House in the hope of getting an interview with the President. A minor Messiah.

Two avant-garde urban architects have finally discovered the last word in modernity. They have rediscovered the medieval borough, with its narrow streets, pedestrians, workshops, artisans, bakers making bread, shopkeepers living above their shops (so that these neighborhoods won't be dead after working hours). The history of this (industrial) civilization is truly bizarre: now it is having to reconstitute, resuscitate everything that it destroyed.

A large portion of this society's vitality has always come from its lack of formal training.

It's clear that there is much more intellectual invention in this country, where pragmatic-empirical idiocy rules, than in the country where ingenious dialectics became the official system.

This great leonine body, riddled with cholera, syphilis and cancer, still majestically dominates the world.

THE END OF THE WORLD
Spectacular beginnings? End of the world? Spectacular beginnings of the end of the world?

ANTHROPOLOGY
A research team has come back from an expedition to Africa whose aim was to find the missing link between apes and Men: "We've found it! It was us . . . "

Civilization, they say, began with the genocide of the Neanderthals. We have an archaic memory within us which, to become conscious, needs to be stimulated by something analogous to what happened in the past. (The key to Platonic reminiscence: the relationship between the brain and DNA).

ANTHROPO-SOCIOLOGY
Against the sociologism that tries to reduce the most universal formulations to their socio-historical conditions (Pascal's *Pensées* "explained" as the product of the *noblesse de robe*); for an anthropologism that interprets every historico-social utterance as a situated and dated bio-anthropological formulation.

THE SOURCE OF HAPPINESS

Delgado floods the nerve centers, calming epilepsy, and *producing* peace, calm, and joy. So here is something much better than narcotics for procuring bliss and ecstasy . . . Will humanity have to concentrate its efforts into escaping from this happiness? Will this become the new opium of the people? (In an episode of *Star Trek, This Side of Paradise*, the cosmonauts force themselves to leave the Eden-like planet. Man (life . . .) *should not* accept too much happiness, just as he should not accept *too much* order).

YOU!

Mentally, I curse *them* (the officials, bureaucrats, managers – and sociology's apprentice official-bureaucrat-managers, the worst of the lot). "You devote so much time to your ceremonial relationships, to your conventional roles, to consolidating your status, to increasing or defending your powers, to your commissions, visits, meetings, tedious dinners, relationships based on interest. And while you are wasting such a huge amount of time, I am busy loving and working. Because I work harder than you! Etc." I get carried away, and denounce the plot in which they are all in league against me (although not all of them were: on the contrary, Aron warned me, Touraine defended me, etc.); I fall back on Bourdieu (every time I breathe, I hurt him, every time I have an idea, he hates me), and I make an improvised psychoanalysis of his hatred for me (though I'm no longer at all sure that I am still the principal object of his obsession or his allergy).

So what's it all about? I am ten thousand kilometers away from *them*, and they come all this way to haunt me? *Raus! Raus! . . . But it's me who's going after them!*

ME

Don't be in too much of a hurry.

EVERYONE

Everyone should learn.

PIGS

At the cinema conference in Aspen, the atmosphere is New Left. At one point, someone in the gallery (where I'm sitting) mentions the militants who have been beaten up or shot by the *pigs*. A guy who looks like a public official, in suit and tie, about forty years old, asks in that case what do we think of the son of a policeman whose father was called a *pig*, and who was killed or injured.

Silence. An embarrassed silence, and an exorcising one no doubt.

And I started thinking. Why do I, too, say *pig*? Why have I always written *pig* in this journal rather than policeman, officer, etc? Of course, the main reason I've used this word is because it's "in". I wouldn't have written cop, for example. But pig is even more sinister than cop. I know, it's nothing like as bad as "dirty Black;" I know, I know, they're the ones who have the power, they *are* repression; I also know that saying cop or pig helps you to resist feeling intimidated. But this term is reductive and degrading, and therefore, however comprehensible, excusable, or helpful it may be, is itself ignoble.

CULTURAL REVOLUTION

As a result of the postwar changes in domestic comfort (apartments and houses with several rooms) and education (the liberalism of the psychoanalytic vulgate), American children are living in a separate world from adults: they have their own bedrooms, complete with symbolic objects and decoration, and this quasi-McLuhanian environment (comics, television) affords them a profoundly autonomous and very intense experience. The modern children of bourgeois America, like children in archaic societies, live in radical segregation from the adult world; only here there is no initiation ritual, institutionalized and organized by adults, to realize their passage into maturity. So these adolescents have had to invent their own initiation, and the most advanced of them, the most tormented, make mortal combat and the confrontation with death a vital part of this new initiation.

Thus self-initiation through poverty, suffering, defiance, aggression, and, in extreme cases, bombings and terrorist attacks, is on the way to becoming an institution.

The similarity with the characteristics of archaic initiation is extraordinary. Just as archaic youths left their villages to go off alone into the terrible forest, modern adolescents go *underground*, into the new ghettoes or the wilderness; just as archaic youths had to face spirits, genies, and ancestors, so modern adolescents go forth to face the *pigs*, and the barbaric gods of the *polis*; just as archaic initiation presupposed torments and bloody trials, modern initiation presupposes the risk of death, either through gambling, or delinquency, or the new urban guerilla. The sole and vital difference is that the archaic institution was entirely controlled by the social hierarchy and the adult class, whereas the new institution which is being created is self-managed by the adolescent class in its desire to achieve adulthood. Insofar as this new initiation is inscribed within revolutionary militancy, does the juvenile class still control the institution, or is it already controlled by some political caste?

The *San Diego Door*, which offered asylum to the *Street Journal* (the former *Free Press*) has been attacked in turn.

The Crisis Center is under threat. A young man in a (drug-induced) coma was transported there. Because he was dying, the Center immediately called the hospital. But a police car accompanied the ambulance, and arrested the dying man's friends. Diana intervened, protested, and she was arrested too.

Here the words *Love*, *Happiness*, *Peace* and *Freedom* have a very powerful, very pure meaning. These are the words that will found the new society and the new religion, which are waiting to be born. *Peace* means not only "Peace in Vietnam" but also: "Let peace be among us," "peace be with you," "I want to be at peace with myself."

The new populism. Since the mob no longer exists, they're transforming themselves into a rustic, shabby, disheveled mob . . .

The Beatles' odyssey: the voyage to India, the search for the guru, drugs, peace, John Lennon and Yoko . . . Their lives are an allegory of the quest that has united the younger generations since 1960. "We are influenced by everything that's happening," says John Lennon (Oh, me too!).

(Mustn't forget to write about the Beatles and the Rolling Stones when I do my paper on the youth revolution).

What's happening here, inside their own minds, is what they believe is happening down there, outside, in Cuba.

Here and now the most profound scientific, technical, moral and anthropological revolution is taking place in California. Yes, I said this before; I am still convinced that it is true.

Last days in San Francisco: our trip coincides with the two explosions in the city and in Berkeley, which injured some policemen. The next day, my friends in Berkeley tell me, a police officer (I no longer say *pig*) stopped a student on Telegraph Avenue. This young man was in the habit of producing his tape recorder in such circumstances; he put the microphone under the police officer's nose, and mockingly began to record him. The police officer took the microphone quite calmly, but then he grabbed the tape recorder, threw it to the ground, smashed it, and trampled it underfoot. Since Monday, the rules have changed, he said.

The bombings were done by "professionals," guys who've come back from Vietnam and know how to make and set bombs.

A new phase has begun.

However, I'm told, these bombings are nothing new, apparently there have been several since the explosion in the Chase Manhattan Bank in New York. In Northern California alone, there are supposed to have been thirty-six explosions in electric power stations. The press, they say, has entered into a conspiracy of silence about these events, at the request of the White House. Is this possible? Are my friends especially well-informed, or are these just rumors making the rounds of radical circles? In any case, they know activist groups in Berkeley that are determined to scale the wall of "re-assimilation." They're impatient, enthusiastic about the urban guerilla.

In fact, it looks as if a permanent guerilla structure will be created in America (which would be clandestine, and violent, staging hold-ups of banks and other capitalist institutions), linked to the Black revolutionary-nationalist underground, but also, in a sense, the successor, among privileged society children, to the "antisocial delinquent gangs" of the 40s and 50s, and, at the political level, the successor to the rebellions "without a cause" of the 50s and 60s.

I am increasingly convinced that if we want to understand all these phenomena, we must recognize that a link exists between the adolescent initiation crisis and the broader crisis of civilization and bourgeois values. Auto-initiation is an expression of this crisis, and an attempt to overcome it. It is increasingly inadequate to let each person initiate himself, haphazardly, slowly, and often incompletely (luckily for some, including myself, unluckily for most others) into the adult social world, and collective initiation is increasingly a necessity. Accordingly, left-wing guerillaism is currently responsible for creating structures of auto-initiation and making them available to these Western bourgeois youngsters – these structures imply the risk of suffering (prison, beatings, even torture) and death, and provide the opportunity to do battle with gods and monsters (the "bourgeoisie," and capital, with their *pigs*). The control of the machinery of initiation by the revolutionary Left, and more extensively by the rebellious segment of the adolescent-juvenile class, is becoming a major phenomenon. In each juvenile generation, the most ardent, the most tormented, and the most eagerly adventurous, will go of their own accord to join the guerilla underground, where they will undergo trials and show what they are made of. What will they be like afterwards? Calmer? Socially integrated? Reformists? Evolutionists? Transformationists? Revolutionaries? Whatever else happens, there is a danger that an urban guerilla will become one wing, one trend, in the vast advancing front of the cultural revolution.

Will this revolution become established, in a circumscribed, localized manner, just as delinquency, gangsterism, and the *cosa nostra* have, without modifying the social structure? Or will it bring a chain reaction in its wake, which will affect this structure in its entirety? And how?

The importance of ecology. I've seen the movement swell, since the article in *Ramparts*, which marked the emergence into the open of a student underground movement. According to my ecologist friends, the new influx of students is much more passionately interested in ecology, and economics, than its predecessor (which was more political in the restricted sense of the term). It's worth noting that ecology also plays a part in the guerilla movement. One of the crimes that the bombing of the Chase Manhattan Bank was supposed to punish was the crime against ecology, meaning the pollution caused by firms under the bank's control. There have been "ecological" actions (and more are being planned) against the big banks which harm Nature.

After dinner in Chinatown, a last immersion in the source, at the Family Dog. Big Brother and a few folk singers are on the program. H. warned me, "It's not like the old days." In the old days, they used to spend their nights at the Fillmore West or at the Family Dog: everybody danced, and sang . . . By the old days, she means just three years ago. And it's true, on this Saturday night everything lacks energy; there's no conviction or inspiration. Nobody's dancing. The youngsters are sitting on the floor, like sad, dutiful children. Here too, gray shabbiness has taken the place of colorful costume.

The next day, very early, H. and D. drive us to the airport. The Gate to the Far West is, naturally, lacquered red, Asian style. We pass through the cordon of flight attendants in kimonos and climb aboard the Japan Air Lines Boeing.

Post-Script
Happiness

Paris, June 1970

A few scattered notes in January, the last, very sparse notes in February . . . It's clear that I've abandoned this journal, partly because I'm forging ahead with my bio-sociological reflection and my meditation on life, but partly also because this combustion has been so all-consuming in the living of it that there is nothing left to be written down, not even a few scraps. What I'd like to do now, long after my return, and in spite of the extreme indiscretion that it requires of me (perhaps also because I'm tempted by its extreme impropriety), is to try and describe what happened, between the middle of December and the middle of February, and which only today, because it is over, can I call by the name I did not dare utter then: happiness.

Rereading the fall pages of this journal, I see that my contentedness, my well-being, is still mingled with anxiety and agitation. However, after mid-December, my anxieties decrease, almost disappear, and I'm less agitated. An amazing thing happened: I gave up smoking, even though I was convinced I'd never be able to stop, because up to then I had only been able to keep off cigarettes when there was a break in routine, if I was in hospital or on holiday; and the feverish state I'm normally in when writing up a book had always kept me bound me to the need to suck in measured quantities of breath: for the past three years, I've smoked whenever I had to write. But at the end of December 1969, when I was right in the middle of my work, writing up the introduction to the *Nature of Society*, I decided to replace cigarettes with a pipe because I was smoking too much, and I don't know how it happened, but although I kept on writing, I gave up cigarettes without even touching the pipe. I was astonished when I realized that I'd freed myself, without exerting my willpower, under the influence of a subterranean will that had gained the upper hand.

It's only today that I can see how far this minor event was a sign of remission from deep within, subtly translated on the surface by the extinction of carbon dioxide fumes and the increasing rarity of my attacks of anxiety. Without really noticing it, I had started to enjoy long stretches, immense stretches of peace, and the moments, hours, even whole days of plenitude flourished within this peace. It was then, and only then, that I began to whisper to myself: "Is this happiness?" I didn't dare answer, even mentally, that it was, for I share the Oriental superstition that you should never admit to good fortune. So I smiled to myself, discreetly, knowingly; when I felt an excess of happiness dangerously close to overflowing, I had recourse to the old ruse. I told myself in a loud and intelligible inner voice: "No, I am not happy."

How did this happiness come about? I know, I feel, that doors within me, sluice-gates, locks, began to open, one after the other, letting in what had always remained outside, freeing the outward flow of what had always remained imprisoned within me, the one (the opening to the outside) being linked to the other (the inner release); and this went on until the day when finally the rusty, bolted gate, the last and the first gate (I think . . .), the one that had never been opened, the one that couldn't be opened, the one that didn't have a key, until the day when it too, suddenly unlocked . . . I can't retrace the chain of events whose fortunate and unconscious plaything I was, when everything happened within me through modifications of pressure and temperature, readjustments, pacifications. Instead, I will try to identify and isolate the combined elements which constituted this happiness.

First there was the joy at being restored to myself. Although in 1962 I'd torn myself away once and for all from the tendrils and temptations of the managerial-academic world, although I had once again sworn fidelity to my own truths, and although I had decided to devote myself entirely to what matters most to me, dissipation, both external and internal, had taken hold of me once again, and I continually had to force myself to push against the wind, or brace myself against it; I hadn't attained peace or the liberty to meditate.

And then when I discovered the unknown continent of new biology, and with it the fundamental problems it has brought to our attention, I suddenly found myself at the heart of my true quest. What is life? What is society? What is Man?

I've been conducting my research at the Salk Institute, in complete freedom, in silence and tranquility. I am disconnected from everything that once preyed on my mind and my life. There are no more "noises off" to prevent me *from listening to the voices that I summon up*. I'm initiating myself, and most of all I have rediscovered the joy of learning, which I forgot so long ago. I read, but not as I did in the preceding decades, when I was always reading at high speed, riding hard to lasso some fact, some idea, which I pursued with some precise goal in mind. Here, at the Salk, I am really cultivating my mind, by which I mean that I'm open to everything I read, I try to soak it up, I read slowly, I reread things that I haven't completely understood two or three times, and I also reread things I like; I don't gulp them down, but chew, savor, enjoy, take pleasure in them. I have rediscovered the great delight which had been lost to me for nearly thirty years, now rendered more exquisite still by the gastronomy and the healthy moderation which has replaced my earlier intellectual gluttony.

The information that I have acquired has gone to work structuring and de-structuring my system of ideas. Whole sections of wall have crumbled, allowing what had been held back behind it suddenly to emerge: the unknown. I reflect, I think, ideas come to me, they multiply, some of them only seem dazzling to me for a moment, and some have become of the greatest importance to me today. For the truth is that the mind works best, not in needlepoint, not in detail, but by thoroughly kneading the clay. The joy and exhilaration of this work, joined with other forms of joy and exhilaration, has also turned into happiness.

And it is all happening in a place like paradise: I love the colors of the earth, the grass, the sea and the sky, I love the desert California and the tropical California, the parched California and the gardened California, I love this other Mediterranean, archetypal in its mild climate and its arid geography, I love the spring which takes the place of fall and winter, I love the permanent sunshine and blue sky, I love the monstrously powerful and playful ocean, I love going to work in jeans and a shirt, I love the low houses, I love the fact that wood and glass take precedence in these houses, the most luxurious of which ostensibly display the signs of rusticity. But what I love the most is that I've been able, in these circumstances, in this place, in this climate, to combine holidays with work. Every day at noon I dive into the ocean; I come back from the Salk, take off my shirt and trousers, buckle my "Olympic" trunks (thus immediately auto-mythologizing myself into a champion, a Triton) while Johanne gets into her swimsuit; I wrap my towel round my waist and we cross the road, go running down the beach, get into the water, screaming with cold, then once we're immersed in it screaming for joy, she floating on the waves, I diving beneath the crests as they tumble over, shaken, tossed about, sometimes an undercurrent knocks me down, usually I come through the liquid wall, swimming up out of it, reborn, exhilarated . . . After the cold, the baking heat, and when this heat lessens, when the cold returns, we get out of the water and run together, chasing each other on the shores, laughing like idiots, happy to be so completely childish . . . We go back across the road; the hot shower floods me with voluptuous pleasure; my body has never enjoyed such a feast of cold, heat, water, air, and sun. It's hungry. We sit down at the table, and enjoy salads of zucchini and carrots cooked in their own juices, at very low heat, or else avocados, papayas . . .

I glance at the sentimental soap opera on TV, which, at this feminine hour, is all about painful love, appalling misunderstandings, false and true friends, nurses, doctors . . . Then I get in my car and head back to the Salk . . .

Except for the times when I can't tear myself away from my reading or writing, I come home at six o'clock, when my science-fiction program begins, and I watch with delight, sensitive to its childish dream-world, its mythico-technological imagination, and the naively profound philosophy it expresses.

We've begun to meet people, at our place, or outside, with friends. Very often, we are blessed with the miracle of a party. But even late at night, I'll spend an hour reading an article or a book that I started at the Salk. So I have verified that happiness does not lie in the separation of holidays and work, but in their union. Holidays and work alternate here, combined and inseparable: my work has all the advantages of holidays, freedom and joy; my telluric, oceanic, solar, cosmic holidays stimulate my work. The joys of this work and of these holidays are both profoundly felt in the depths of my being.

Our house is both the obvious and the magical setting for this double life. It looks out onto the sea, from which it is only separated by the road. Poised lightly on the ground, it's like some wonderful holiday bungalow. At the same time, it's a real home, so comfortable and well-appointed. I like the fact that it is not designed to take root in time, but to adapt to the moment. With its three bathrooms, the kitchen with its nine appliances, the wood interior, which is so gentle on the eye, the patios, the bay windows overlooking the sea, it's my "ideal home." And since mid-December it has become home to our temporary family; we were amazed that six, seven, eight of us could live together, at very close quarters and yet with so much space, without getting in one another's way, without bothering about the washing up, without having to wait to use the toilet or the bathtub.

I could live here forever. I feel more at home here than anywhere else, even though it's in La Jolla, this dead, grim, very residential neighborhood. But we soon stopped thinking of this neighborhood as our environment; our real environment is the youngsters from the campus who come to surf or daydream on our shores, and our friends whose homes mark off our territory and whom we meet all the time, it's the Salk Institute and the University, it's the Californian land.

I am so happy to be in California. It's not only the geo-climatic euphoria of the new Eldorado, it's also the exaltation of knowing and feeling myself to be inside the brain of the spaceship earth, to be living as a witness to this crucial moment in the anthropological adventure. Of course, I'm aware that death and disaster are on the prowl, but they cannot be dissociated from rebirth and infinite hope. I am, as always, galvanized by everything that represents a return to the primordial chaos. Here I have found my place: it's here that the new possible worlds are being forged, that the trophic forces of humanity are emerging, and that what in my exaltation I could call the biological Genius, or the Being-in-becoming-of-the-world, is fermenting. The problems that interest me are *alive* here. Everything that is taking shape and being experimented has penetrated me by osmosis, and is nourishing me. Everything that I find beautiful and admirable gives me the vitamins I need to make progress, to improve myself . . .

And so once more I find myself engaged in my singular quest for a truth which would be the truth of my existence, for a wisdom which would be my life's wisdom, for an answer to my fundamental need.

This need will be fulfilled here, more amply and more durably than before or elsewhere; I could call it *aimance,*[34] a term which envelops, confuses and intermingles the words *amour* and *amitié*[35] in the loving relationship with others, where the friend is more than a friend: he or she is also beloved; and where the woman I love is absolutely my friend; *aimance* also signifies the search for a life which would be permanently ruled by the magnetic force bringing together people who are attracted to one another.

And that's what has happened: a wonderful, warm, magnetic network was established, and it grew slowly, imperceptibly, until by December we were curled up in a placenta of friendship, tenderly united with about twenty people, some of whom have already been mentioned in this journal, and others whose names have never appeared here, although they were so much a part of to our lives: Marie-Christine and Russell, Bibi and her judge, the Mac A.s, Marylou and Bob, Austryn and Michèle, Pamela and Robert. We spent affectionate evenings together, laughing and dancing. When we danced it wasn't as a pretext for the kind of flirtatious caresses which mark the end of parties and the beginning of orgies; it was the expression and realization of our exhilaration and our joy to be living together.

We broke the mold of formal receptions and stuffy dinner parties. But much more importantly, our irruption as a couple among those who became our friends awoke a voice in them: "*It's time to be what you are.*" Everyone felt the need to get more in touch with themselves, and some felt inspired to change their lives. In a sense we were the *theoremic*[36] couple, whose appearance changed everybody and brought them back to themselves.

But our theoremic action never went as far as sexual love and our "love parties" never ended in bodily union. There was a line we never crossed, a dissociation of tenderness and sex, a no man's land between our union in loving friendship and an engagement in sexual union. To cross that line, we would all have had to get over fairly radical insecurities, and overcome the possibility of jealousy; in short, we would have already had to have arrived at the end of the road down which we had only just set forth.

But we did cross a different line, the one that took us into our new "family." We only took the first step, but still this step was taken: a little community formed in our house, for two periods of three weeks, first of all with Véro, Françoise, André, and Evelyne, and a second time with Vidal, Corinne, Alanys, and to a certain extent Ellen, and this little community was more than the mere cohabitation of friends and relatives on holiday; it was already a trial run, our first experience of the kind of "family" whose basis was both kinship and friendship, but which went beyond either of them. Beginning in December, there was an osmosis, a mutual integration between each one of us and between all of us. I felt it, we all felt it, because of the extraordinary, tranquil happiness of which we all had a taste, and which all of us – I, Véro, the Burgs, Françoise – enjoyed together, culminating in our drive through the desert in the station wagon.

At the center of gravity and at the source of this *aimance*, and at my center of gravity and my source, there is Johanne. Johanne is the comet of love who sweeps all of us along in her train. She is the great communicator, going up to everybody, wanting to know them, opening them up, diving down into them. She has amazed me so many times, first by striking up conversations with such dull creatures, and then by bringing out their unsuspected qualities. It is Johanne who inspires and reveals what is best in everyone. Her primal wound has become a fountain. Johanne hemorrhages love, she loves making gifts, spreads them all around her, she gives, she gives herself, and her generosity results in more gifts; presents multiply in all directions. My Californian happiness is primarily the gift that Johanne made of it to me.

At Johanne's side, and as close as possible between us, for a few weeks, there was Alanys.

I admire both of them; they are so profoundly alike and unalike, the Black woman and the Indian, both of mixed race, both abandoned and adopted, both of them rejected and loved, children of sorrow and creatures of joy, both queens, strangers, present everywhere, extra-lucid; they are animals, goddess-children; Johanne is always exuberant, a crazy dog fervently licking every hand, any hand dangling within her reach, Alanys is reserved at first, silent, on the defensive, Johanne closer to laughter, Alanys closer to tears, both of them always close to laughter and ready to laugh until they cry . . . Johanne the cosmopolitan, intermittently a Black or a White Canadian woman, or tropical, turning Magyar, Japanese, Lusitanian, Maghribi, with a chameleon-like mimicry that allows her to adapt to and escape from every environment; Alanys devoted to the service of the Indian people, fiercely and tenderly affirming her roots in the proudest and most despised of identities; Johanne scattering herself in the winds, forgetting herself in the moment, enjoying every moment; Alanys the militant, working for the cause of her brothers, singing in the reservations and in the prisons.

I was amazed to discover that love does not alter love; that love is verified, that it flourishes, in abundance and not penury. I felt that pure love, I mean a love without additives, coagulants or artificial rising agents, comes not only from our need to love, but also from the beauty of the entire person whom we find loveable (and not just from her face or her body). Thus, the heat that burns in my veins does not only come from my central fire, but from the radiance of these solar creatures. Love is not only my subjective need. It imposes itself upon me with objective, majestic, gravitational necessity. (Of course, there must also be a harmony of vibrations, a compatibility of smiles, glances, skin . . .). Therefore I loved Johanne, I loved Alanys, and I was also attracted, that February, to Elisabeth and Colette, and three months later in Lisbon, I also loved my solar Luna . . . What in the past had been my juvenile tendency to fall in love on the promise of a face has become my polyphonic ability to love the creatures who embody the qualities I admire.

One evening in February, exhilarated by my thoughts of all these beautiful women, I wrote:

You are illuminated by
my distant love,
dead, immemorial,
You, my living beloved

You are brilliant, you are many
Now that the first star has died
And her light streams forth to make a Milky Way.

There is something incomprehensible in this poem, unless you know about the extraordinary event that took place that February, and which I believe, I hope, brought peace to the depths of my being . . .

The great pacification had begun before my departure for California. V. loved and was loved by a man that I admire, and our relationship did not come to an end as a result, but was reconstituted; it improved. My daughters, I and Véro got over their troubles and the grief they had felt over our separation eight years ago, and a natural dialogue replaced the silence full of unspoken words which had been weighing on our relationship. So when I left for San Diego I was already free from the clutches of Worry and Guilt, which had spoiled my joys until then, and this was certainly the necessary and preliminary condition for my happiness. Indeed, this happiness began as soon as I and Véro landed in San Diego.

I'd invited them for the end-of-the-year festivities, and they arrived on a charter flight with André and Evelyne. It wasn't just that I was happy to form a family with the girls and their friends. I was happy to find myself in the same house as them, after so many years, and happy that they should be under my roof. I was happy to live with them for a while. I believed I had finally found peace.

But this was not yet my final peace. Something else had to happen before my happiness could blossom as it blossomed afterwards: an unpredictable and unexpected event, the opening of the secret door.

To make what I am going to say understandable, I would almost have to tell the story of my whole life, going all the way back to the family *Arkhe*, and tell a part of the story that does not belong to me alone – and which therefore I cannot disclose. I will only remind my readers that my mother died when I was just ten years old. Her name was Luna, like the planet which, according to my horoscope, lights up my sky and provides my ascendant sign. This accident profoundly disturbed my relationship with my father and with my family, and thus with myself. My father, Vidal, loved, and, after many difficulties, married my mother's younger sister, Corinne, a woman born to be happy, but who, after my mother's death, suffered a terrible inner distress which ruined her health without ever altering her loving and curious nature.

After I freed myself, thanks to the war that saved my life while it destroyed millions of other young men, I began to recognize my father's qualities; I admired him, I appreciated his candor, and his love of laughter which so precisely expresses his love of life, still intact despite the extraordinary sorrows, worries and ill fortune he has had to face. Yes, with every passing year, I loved my father a little more: I mean I respected him a little more, recognized him a little better (for the modern problem is not to be recognized by one's father, but to recognize him).

In short, I thought that everything had been resolved and laid to rest several years ago. Better than laid to rest, in fact, because Johanne contributed an affection which brought us all closer to each other. Everything was fine. There was still something very strange in my behavior towards my parents, but I refused to pay any attention to it. I avoided spending too much time with them; as soon as the Wednesday night dinner was finished, I got away as quickly as I could. Although I love Corinne's extremely light Sephardic cooking more than anything, I had trouble digesting it. I was almost never completely relaxed with them; most of the time I was irritable, agitated. Johanne sometimes reproached me for being disagreeable, and in fact I was often surprised by it myself, but I couldn't change anything and I would forget all about it as soon as I could. I just couldn't get beyond the realization that my father annoyed me. He sometimes annoyed me for a reason, but usually there was no cause for it at all. This allergy, too, seemed natural to me. Partly because it's the same for many sons or daughters with respect to their father or mother, and I know that families are our favorite places for getting annoyed with each other.

And partly because I had summarily psychoanalyzed the entire affair, and I clearly saw the source of my allergy. This semi-lucidity therefore helped to blind me to my problem, because it helped to make me recognize the abnormality of my behavior as being the natural result of my Oedipal story. In January 1970, while we were in La Jolla, my father and Corinne both fell ill, he from extreme fatigue, and she from an attack of depression. Ordinarily, my father always concealed his troubles and his illnesses while he had them, and only told me about them afterwards.

For the first time in his life, and in mine, he sent me an anxious letter, asking me to give up my plans to return via Asia and come back earlier to Europe. He wants the four of us to go to Ravello, where Johanne and I invited them to come and join us two years beforehand.

This letter makes a great impression on me. It isn't because I'm worried about his health, it's because I've received my father's first call for help: because I feel for the first time that he is *old*. The realization of my father's mortality is a huge leap forward. I telephone Paris at once and invite them to come and stay with us in San Diego.

My father is terrified of the plane journey, but since this fear does not constitute a reasonable objection, he raises the problem of money. I reply that TWA has recently started offering special bargain-price tickets, and that anyway I can cover the expenses of their journey. "In that case, give me the money to go to Ravello," he says, in a final attempt at escape. "No way, old man!" Corinne, who is listening in, is enthusiastic. I hear her cry "Yes, yes, come on, let's go." He argues, "We'll see, let me think about it." When I put the phone down, I haven't managed to get a firm promise out of him. Will they come? Two days later I receive a telegram announcing the day and time of their flight. Another phone call, and I learn that, since we invited them, Corinne has recovered from her problems and her insomnia. For my part, great waves of joy wash over me every day. What emerges into my conscious mind, in these moments, is the idea that for the first time in my life, having always received things from my father without ever giving him anything, I am giving him a present. And having never lived under the same roof with him since the time of my emancipation, I am offering him my home, and America, California, a rest, peace . . . I can thank him before it's too late. I get ready to enjoy every minute of this stay together as my most delicious reward. I feel so happy, but at the same time I'm anxious and oppressed once more; I have sudden attacks of irritation at Johanne, and, as the great day approaches, my joy and my anxiety are both increasing. The night before their arrival, I dream that my mother comes back. I'm in the street, in Paris, I am my current age, and I know that I have to go on holiday with Vidal and Corinne. I suddenly find out, I don't know how, that my mother has come back. This event starts off being a harmless piece of news, but the information grows, swells, becomes more and more overwhelming. I start running. I think: "I'll go and tell Johanne that I'm going to stay the night with my mother, she'll understand." I run, hurrying faster and faster, I panic, and my panic wrenches me out of my sleep. I'm still caught up in the excitement of the dream, my heart is desperately leaping out towards my mother, while at the same time the cruel, icy realization is rushing down on me that it's only a dream, that my mother is dead, that she hasn't come back. I burst into tears, cry out, start to scream; Johanne wakes up, puts her arms around me, tries to understand, but I can't tell her anything yet. When I've calmed down, I slowly begin to recognize my dream, this dream which was a daily occurrence in my childhood, but was buried under the weight of four decades, disappeared, forgotten, lost, and which has only reappeared now, when I'm forty-eight years old! I explain all this to Johanne, with the most profound grief; I suddenly find that I'm extraordinarily tired, and I fall back into a deep sleep. When I wake up the next morning, I feel good, pacified and happy, and I realize that I have finally understood the whole thing. I've understood that until I was forty-eight years old, and with astonishing tenacity, something primitive within me had clung to the hope that my mother would come back, and that it was ill every time I saw my father. This thing in me had not yet admitted the facts, not for the reasons that I had always given myself before, but because accepting them would have meant that my mother was truly dead, that she would never come back again. What an incredible ruse of hope, or of despair, it's impossible to say . . . In any case I'd had to wait until this night, in La Jolla, to assimilate the truth completely. This awakening in tears was not only the feeling I'd had every morning at the age of ten, eleven, twelve, thirteen, and more: sorrow at the discovery that my mother was dead, a sorrow submerged by the dream of the preceding night in the renewed revival of my hope for her return, for like Prince Sigismond,[37] I was living then in alternation between the nightmare of reality and the reality of the dream. And now my mourning was finally over; this was the final rent, the final wrench at a bloody fetus, the penetration of cold light into the last and deepest hiding place where it had never before managed to penetrate. The shock and aftershock of the dream and the awakening was caused by a subterranean explosion opening the final breach. Now I knew that she would not be coming back, and this "she would not be coming back" caused me the most terrible, ultimate grief, but also brought me true peace at last.

With this central piece of the puzzle, I could at last reconstitute the entire story of my life, and look at everything that I had neglected and repressed in the face. But to tell the truth, even before I had recapitulated, reflected, and reconstituted, I knew as soon as I woke up, that morning, that this time it would all be all right, that my father would not annoy me, that from now on I could spend weeks close to him, close to them, with them, in happiness and serenity.

This was as good as psychoanalysis. It was, in fact, similar to the liberating trauma at the end of an analysis; a catharsis resulting from the final and crucial repetition of the event to which I had unconsciously remained a prisoner. I was very proud that this had happened to me after my interminable efforts to know and recognize myself. The act that liberated me was, in the end, the acceptance of my mother's death, of course, but it was also the acceptance of the death of my insane hopes, and perhaps the acceptance of *death* itself . . .

A complete, incredible happiness was my immediate recompense. Everything went as well as it could, during the three weeks we spent together, for all of us and for each one of us, exactly as I had known it would when I awoke on the day of their arrival. At the same time, Alanys was there, a supplement as gratuitous as she was necessary: this month of February brought about the full bloom of everything that had been preparing to flower since the end of December. The youthful faces we met on the shores smiled at us as if they could read peace and love on our own faces. We exchanged the two-fingered sign. *Peace*! *Love*! It was a succession of joys, connecting, whirling: reading, studying, writing, diving, running, showering; the immense ocean, rumbling and good; the sovereign, dramatic sun; the streaming moon; the loving evenings, intoxicated, exuberant, dancing. We kept putting the same records back on the turntable: *Fool on the Hill*, *Ode to Billy Joe* sung by Bobby Gentry, *On the Bayou* and *Graveyard Train* by Credence Clearwater Revival, and we were in ecstasy.

I was constantly high without needing grass or alcohol, but always ready to take them when offered. All our pleasures thus intensified became voluptuous, all our joys became happiness. I could no longer express anything in my journal, I could only exclaim, and not write. I just noted this: "I am savoring drops of life. I am dripping with lust for life."[38] Sometimes I felt I was being suffocated by nothing, by which I mean by Everything. Everything was in the most insignificant little thing, and the most insignificant little thing was too much, too intense, too good. I had experienced extraordinary ecstasy, insane joy before, but never, never, had I experienced such happiness.

At the age of forty-eight, I lived life to the full for a season. Is this normal? Abnormal? Did I pay too dearly for it? Was it a miracle? In any case, I knew that my happiness was temporary, that it depended on an extraordinary combination of circumstances, that it would evaporate one day, and soon. But this happiness was not only a providential oasis; I knew that its ebb would leave me with something new, I knew that the great reconciliation of which it was the harvest also corresponded to a battle I had won.

I told myself, with astonishment: "At the age of forty-eight, I'm learning how to live!" On the one hand, I was sorry that so much time had had to pass before this crucial point had been reached, and I was sad to think that I would not be able to live the two centuries I would need to fulfil the promises of my nearly fifty-year adolescence. But on the other hand, I felt that I was privileged, for most so-called adults are atrophied creatures, mutilated and deficient, ignorant of the misery of their arrested development. And most of all, what voluptuousness, what delight to feel myself capable of progressing, understanding better, becoming more open, more loving . . .

I wrote: "I'm learning, tasting, enjoying, loving, seeking." This was the formula for the completeness of my happiness. On the one hand it was the happiness related to curiosity, questioning, and seeking; on the other it was the happiness related to love. Love has always been my maxim, haunting, senile, infantile, obscene, and ridiculous; but despite my acute awareness of this ridiculousness, obscenity, infantilism and senility, it remains my irrepressible truth. I have always loved humanity, my friends, a woman-companion, a woman-idol, but now love has become less abstract, less narcissistic, less tormented, less painful, and all this without losing its force; on the contrary, it's because it was set free, because it was opened outward. For example, my love of the universal is no longer merely ideal, it has become a concrete love for the universe: on our return from California, stopping in Japan, Cambodia, and Ceylon, I felt more strongly than ever that every culture, every ethnicity in the world has something specifically loveable about it; I don't mean the museums and mausoleums, but the food, the different provinces, faces, and colors. Of course, in each country I tried to take my sociological bearings, to study the problem of development, and seek out the avant-garde, but above all I started to fall in love with each people, with each culture, and in Kandy I suddenly cried to Johanne (it doesn't matter if it was after a curry, after watching the Magul Bera dance, after I don't know what else): "I'm in love with the world!"

I'm quite aware, as I write these lines, that some people will object: can one be happy in an under-developed country, can one be happy in a suffering world? But this question is hardly put in adequate terms. America is not only the country of imperialism, but also that of the youth crusade; Asia is not only under-development, but also fabulous cultural wealth; the world is not only suffering, but also search and experience. More profoundly, one might ask: if happiness is linked to love, must we prevent ourselves from loving? If happiness is linked to progress, must we renounce all personal progress? If happiness is the fruit of a long and hazardous journey, must we refuse the march and the trials in order to avoid all risk of happiness? And what if happiness is produced by a distillation, a quintessence, of suffering?[39] What then? . . . Must we avoid suffering in order to avoid being happy? But why am I trying to convince the new inquisitors? It's enough for me to know that only our personal progress can contribute, in a non-deceptive and infallible way, to general progress. This is the idea that I want to pass on, that I must pass on, if it's possible to pass on an experience which took forty-eight years to take form.

I see quite clearly that all my inner efforts toward exoneration, self-knowledge, self-liberation, and self-improvement could not have been decisive on their own. It also took a meeting, an event, luck.

Luck itself undoubtedly has Johanne's face, but its name is also California, where the conditions for what was both my progress and my happiness were at last, incredibly, united. There, in California, I recognized the unity of my research and I set off again on my essential quest. It was in this entranced land that I drank from mouth to mouth the renascent message of a very ancient gospel, *Love, Peace.* It was in California that I was finally able to rediscover my family, and bring others into my family circle.

It was in California that an extraordinary season of my life began and ended. In 1962, Woe befell me on the Golden Gate Bridge. I did not know then that I was already on the road to Larkspur. And it is from Larkspur that I am now leaving America, having returned eight years later. Once again I am crossing that sublime bridge, early in the morning, in the brilliant light of the rising sun.

Notes

1 Translator's Note: *La Connaissance de la connaisance* (volume 3 of Morin's *La Méthode*) was published in 1986 (Paris, Seuil).

2 T.N.: Svetlana Alliluyeva, the daughter of Stalin, who had emigrated to the United States in March 1967 in a much-publicized defection that was used for the propaganda purposes of the West during this phase of the Cold War. She later returned to the Soviet Union in November 1984, attacking Western "pseudo-democracy", but again fled to the U.S. in 1986.

3 T.N.: In English in the text.

4 T.N.: Tom Hayden, Leftist leader and member of the "Chicago Seven", who would later become an assemblyman in the California State Legislature.

5 T.N.: Jacques Monod (1910–1976) was a French biochemist, who won the Nobel prize for medicine in 1965 (with F. Jacob and A. Lwoff) for his work on the biochemical mechanisms of the transmission of genetic information.

6 T.N.: Philip Blaiberg was the second person to survive a human heart transplant operation; the operation was performed in Capetown, South Africa by Dr. Christiaan Barnard in 1968.

7 T.N.: "thinking rooms". The affix "oir" indicates a room or place in which something is done, e.g. "pissoir," urinal; the laboratories probably resemble "pissoirs" to a certain extent, with porcelain sinks, etc.

8 T.N.: American psychosociologists of German and Romanian origin respectively, who studied group dynamics.

9 T.N.:"Putanisme" is a neologism based on the word "putain," prostitute, commonly used as an oath. The neologism's proximity to "puritanisme" combines debauched dissipation with its apparent opposite, and thus suggests that the two terms are not necessarily mutually exclusive.

10 T.N.: Pierre Teilhard de Chardin, the French theologian, philosopher and paleontologist, attempted through his optimistic evolutionism to reconcile the demands of science with those of Catholicism.

11 T.N.: "Génie" means genius, spirit, genie, even engineer. Its proximity to "gène" (gene) is important; the English "genius" preserves this relation.

12 T.N.: Morin's neologism is "événementialisé."

13 T.N. *Le Vif du sujet* was published by Seuil in 1969.

14 T.N.: Morin's heading, "L'inculte de la personnalité", is an untranslatable play on words: "inculte" means uneducated, ignorant; the pun is based on the fact that "culte" also means "cult."

15 T.N.: Morin's term is "la pensée alternative." "Alternative" does not mean "unconventional" here, but refers to the type of thinking that promotes or attempts to eliminate one term of a pair in opposition: "either x or y."

16 T.N.: Morin's *L'homme et la mort* was first published in 1951 (Paris, Buchet et Chastel); there was in fact a second edition in 1970, and a third in 1976 (both Paris, Seuil).

17 T.N.: James D. Watson, *The Double Helix: a personal account of the discovery of the structure of D.N.A.* The quotations which follow are taken from the Atheneum edition, New York, 1968.

18 E.g. the ethology of Konrad Lorenz, etc., and especially the research conducted in the last ten years on groups of monkeys (baboons, chimpanzees, no longer in cages, but free (under observation)). Crichton and Benedict said some interesting things. I didn't quite grasp how Crichton arrives at the conclusion that the social bond between baboons is based, not on sexual domination, but on a domination that is, so to speak, pre-political.

19 T.N.: Both "self" and "me" are in English in the text.

20 T.N.: ADN is the French for DNA

21 The writers and artists of the "beat generation," and more extensively the bohemian fringes of the intelligentsia

22 T.N.: "Sous policé ou sous-policisé," in the text. "Sous," under, "policé," culturally refined; "policisé," a neologism (there is no equivalent verb in French for the English "to police"); both derive from the same etymological root: the Greek "politeia," meaning the art of governing the "polis," or city.

23 T.N.: Andrey Donatovich Sinyavsky and Yuly Daniel were convicted of producing anti-Soviet propaganda in February 1966. Both were sentenced to hard labor, and their trial prompted domestic and international protest. Sinyavsky taught Russian Literature at the Sorbonne after his release in 1971.

24 T.N.: Andrei Alexandrovitch Jdanov (1896–1948) was named third secretary of the Soviet Communist Party in 1946, and was one of the principal defenders of Stalinist orthodoxy in literature, philosophy and the arts as well as in the political, social and economic domains. He contributed to the creation of the Komintern in 1947.

25 It could perhaps assimilate its mystical and community-oriented vigor . . .

26 T.N. *Rumour in Orleans* is the title of the translation (P. Green, London, Blond, 1971) of Morin's *La Rumeur d'Orléans* (Seuil, 1969).

27 T.N: The impersonal verb "falloir" has the same etymological root (the Latin "fallere") as the English "fault," in the archaic sense of deficiency or lack of something. "Il faut" has several meanings, expressing need, obligation, and fatality.

28 T.N.: This English version of the text is taken from *The Collected Works of Spinoza, volume 1*, pp. 8–10, edited and translated by Edwin Curley, Princeton University Press, Princeton New Jersey, 1985.

29 T.N.: A Marsupilami is a child's rubber-and-wire toy, based on the cartoons of Spirou. The name is a contraction of "marsupial" and "ami," friend.

30 For her part, Stephanie Mills voices the new link between demography and revolution: "We are fighting for less maternity and more fraternity."

31 The "New Left" is only an embryo, and for the most part a regressive one, in the belly of the new politics which is attempting to establish its identity.

32 T.N.: The pit at Padirac, in the Lot region of France, is over 200 feet deep and leads to an underground river.

33 T.N.: Carl Rogers, prominent humanistic psychologist, whose Center for Studies of the Person was based in La Jolla.
34 T.N: this neologism, with the combined connotations of "aimant," adjective, meaning "loving," and "aimant," noun, meaning "magnet" evokes a kind of love formed on the basis of instinctive attraction.
35 T.N: "amour," love; "amitié," friendship.
36 T.N.: cf. Pasolini's film *Theorem.*
37 T.N.: The hero of Calderón's *La Vida es sueño.*
38 T.N.: the text reads: "Je goûte des gouttes de vie. Je goutte du goût de vivre."
39 Here is the idea that occurred to me, even later, after lunching with M. Both wines we had were excellent, and I kept thinking about the pleasure they had given me a long time after leaving the table. I told myself that when I was twenty, I wouldn't have enjoyed drinking good wine as much, but neither would I have felt displeasure at drinking bad wine. And suddenly I was able to formulate a philosophy gleaned from this experience. What is sensitivity? It is being able to experience greater pleasure and greater suffering. My sensitivity as an oenophile has increased, and therefore I experience greater pleasure (from good wine) and I suffer greater displeasure (from bad wine). Hence my powerful intuition of a great anthropo-biological truth: dd.